THE SECRET OF
A GREAT INFLUENCE

THE SECRET OF
A GREAT INFLUENCE

NOTES ON
BISHOP WESTCOTT'S TEACHING

BY

Mrs. HORACE PORTER

WITH A CHAPTER ON

BISHOP WESTCOTT'S COMMENTARIES

BY THE

Rev. ARTHUR WESTCOTT

London
MACMILLAN AND CO., Limited
NEW YORK : THE MACMILLAN COMPANY

1905

PREFACE

IT often happens that when the first and worthiest tributes have been laid upon a master's grave, some humble disciple will venture to draw near with a poor token only redeemed from worthlessness by the love that has given of its best. He will follow a long way after the rest, and with much halting; now held back by the fear of seeming overbold; now urged on by a gratitude that will not be denied expression.

In much the same way have I hesitated between a longing to find some way of trying to acknowledge the debt I owe to Bishop Westcott's teaching, and the painful consciousness of lack of power to do so worthily. Gratitude at last has won the day, and in these pages I have tried to gather together some of the treasures of stronger faith, and wider hope, and clearer vision which the Bishop's writings offer to those who will seek them there. The fact that through his writings only have I been able to learn of this great teacher may be an added encouragement to others in the same position.

The circle of Bishop Westcott's readers is widening every day. It will increase more and more, the more clearly it is recognised that the truths with which he deals are not for scholars and students only, but offer the most practical help in even the busiest lives. To show this plainly is the purpose of this book, and not to attempt the needless task of calling attention to the Bishop's distinguished scholarship. At the same time, to leave this wholly out of sight would be to give a misleading impression of his influence. I am therefore deeply grateful to the Rev. Arthur Westcott for the Chapter he has kindly added on the *Commentaries*, which have won for the Bishop his high place in the world of scholars.

The writing of this book has been at once a joy and a discipline. A joy, because the retracing of the familiar lines of thought has given them fresh force. A discipline, because no impatient, careless, or self-seeking work could be offered to the memory of one whose whole life was a lesson on the hallowing of endeavour.

MARY PORTER.

December 1904.

CONTENTS

I

BISHOP WESTCOTT'S LIFE-WORK

BISHOP WESTCOTT'S LIFE-WORK

"To make of life one harmonious whole, to realise the invisible, to anticipate the transfiguring majesty of the Divine Presence, is all that is worth living for."—*Christian Aspects*.

"Life is first a sacrifice, and then it is a miracle."—*Characteristics of the Gospel Miracles*.

THERE is always something attractive in the thought of personal influence, personal power. The whole succession of so-called scientific religions, or spiritual sciences, that come into vogue under the guise of novelty, owe their following to the offer which they one and all make to their disciples, of enabling them to gain a greater measure of personal attraction, influence, force. Our first question, when we meet with a life of unusual power, is to ask its secret. If we can learn that, we may be able at least in some degree to emulate the result.

In Bishop Westcott's life and writings, we are face to face with a splendid example of a strikingly deep and far-reaching influence over the hearts and lives of men and women of widely differing gifts and circumstances. Before we can decide upon its value to ourselves, we shall want to know, first and foremost, what were the natural gifts at his command.

3

He was a fine scholar—one of the finest of his day—yet we know all too well, by many examples, that scholarship does not necessarily win hearts, far less draw souls to God.

He was a great writer, but a difficult one, at times, to follow. His was not a simple style, and his thoughts were too deep to be conveyed in easy phrases. His books have often been described, with a great measure of truth, as "ideal," or "mystical." "Obscure" they are sometimes also called, with less appropriateness ; "indistinct from the excess of light"—to borrow one of his own phrases—would be a truer description.

He was a devoted and most thorough student of social problems ; but here also he dealt far more with unattainable ideals than with practical, definite suggestions. His efforts, in every department of his work, have frequently been summed up as deeply intellectual and spiritual, but visionary, impracticable, vague.

So much for the verdict of observation ; what do we find by appealing to results? We see student after student led by this scholarship to offer up intellect as well as heart to God's service, with a consecration of which before they had not dreamed. We see these books, with all their difficulties, helping an ever-widening circle of readers to gain a clearer vision of the glories of this world, and the powers of the world to come. And from not one source only, but many, come evidences of the practical results wrought by those high ideals. In the attitude of the Durham miners, for instance, during the labour warfare, and in the respect and confidence they consistently displayed towards the Bishop, we have a striking token of the value of the lofty visions of Christian brotherhood he had so steadfastly kept before himself and them. While the annals of missionary effort record few greater triumphs of personal influence than the letter in which the younger clergy of his diocese placed themselves unreservedly under his direction, for home or foreign service.[1]

As the Master of Trinity has said of the last sermon which the Bishop preached at Cambridge :[2] "No man had ever a better right to use the words with which he then took leave of us—'The world is ruled by great ideals ; the soul responds to them.'"

Such, then, was and is Bishop Westcott's power —his penetrating, widespread influence—next, as to its secret. And here lies the special charm and value of his life, that this secret is an open one, within the reach of everybody to master. With many a great personality, the secret of power is something complex, intangible, that seems to die with its possessor. With Bishop Westcott it is not so. The two most characteristic features of his wonderful influence are—first, the force with which it lives on after his death, and next, the absolute unanimity with which it is described by all who knew him. It was the power of a life lived wholly and unreservedly by the light of things eternal and unseen ; and no one could come in contact with him without recognising it as such.

[1] See *Lessons from Work*, Appendix.
[2] See *Christian Aspects of Life*.

" What we treasure above all "—wrote his eldest son [1]—" is the unspeakable heritage of a life which was daily lived before our eyes upon the loftiest plane of Christian principle. . . . My father's was a devotion on what may truthfully be called the very grandest scale . . . To all who came near to him, the irresistible truth was certainly brought home, that here was a servant of Christ who served Him every day and all the day."

In the same way Archdeacon Boutflower [2] has summed up the close personal knowledge gained by his eleven years' chaplaincy.[3]

" In the presence of the unseen he met all life, and you could not surprise him out of it. In this atmosphere he worked and breathed. Not only God Himself, but the cloud of witnesses, the communion of the unseen Body of Christ, were more real to him than things seen. . . . He told more than one friend that, when his youngest son died in India, it seemed to him as though he was given back to them in nearness now that the barrier of space was removed by death."

And again—and here we touch the very heart of the secret—" He was only strong because he *saw*, and took time to see."

Precisely the same is the witness of Canon Scott Holland, written of his experience as a pupil, in the earlier Peterborough days :

" The first interview revealed where the secret of his power lay. We had never before seen such an identification of study with prayer. He read and

---

[1] *Life of Bishop Westcott*, Introduction.
[2] Now Bishop of Dorking.   [3] *Life of Bishop Westcott.*

worked in the very mind in which he prayed ; and his prayer was of singular intensity. It might be only the elements of textual criticism with which he was dealing ; but still, it was all steeped in the atmosphere of awe, and devotion, and mystery, and consecration. He taught as one who ministered at an Altar ; and the details of the sacred Text were to him as the Ritual of some Sacramental Action." [1]

It is a striking thing, this unvarying testimony from the most different witnesses to the penetrating influence of a soul turned ever towards its God. The spiritual power could not fail of being understood, however hard the intellectual flights might be to follow. Speaking of Dr. Westcott's gatherings of undergraduates at Cambridge, one who often attended them did not hesitate to assert that "whether we understood him or not, we always felt that we were in the presence of a saint, and that it did us good to see and hear him." [2]

So also Canon Scott Holland has said of one of the Bishop's later addresses :

"The real and vital impression made came from the intensity of the spiritual passion which forced itself out through that strangely knotted brow, and lit up those wonderful grey eyes, and shook that thin, high voice into some ringing clang as of a trumpet. There was a famous address, at the founding of the Christian Social Union . . . which none who were present can ever forget. Yet none of us can ever recall, in the least, what was said. No one knows. Only we know that we were lifted, kindled, transformed. . . . Words had become only symbols.

[1] *Life of Bishop Westcott.* [2] *Ibid.*

There was nothing verbal to report or to repeat. We could remember nothing except the spirit which was in the words : and that was enough." [1]

This was the splendid tribute won from his generation by one of the foremost scholars of the day ; that it is always of his saintship rather than of his scholarship that his friends delight to speak. As another of them wrote : " He laid his great literary gifts at the foot of the Cross " ; and the mark of consecration was never absent from them.

Here we have also the secret of the power by which his books have influenced, and still are influencing, thousands who have never seen him— the recognised presence of a faith to which things unseen and eternal and divine are closer and more real than the things of time and sense. It is the power by which one rapt and reverent worshipper can recall a crowd of inattentive dreamers to the Presence of God. As indeed, of Bishop Westcott himself it has been said that the sight of his countenance in church would transform the simplest service into a true act of worship in fellowship with angels and archangels, and all the company of Heaven.

A power it is, surely, abundantly worth studying; especially in these days when the longing for personal power of all kinds leads so many to seek for it in what the Bishop himself called " strange and unhallowed ways." In him we have one who attained to a striking measure of influence, which death has not destroyed ; and his way thereto lay in simply looking upon all life, work, study, worship,

[1] *Life of Bishop Westcott.*

sorrow, joy, and even human love itself, as different veils or revelations through which to gain glimpses, more or less imperfect, of the majesty and love of God. His whole life—and therein lay at once its strength and its serenity—consisted in one single effort made by different means to attain to a clearer vision of the glory of the eternal God, revealed in our Lord Jesus Christ, and brought home to the soul by the Holy Spirit. And the result was that stead-fast purpose and unbroken peace which many of us contrast so sadly with our own fragmentary lives of warring desires and clashing duties, confused by the restlessness which the Bishop has described in a passage that speaks to many hearts :

"Must we not confess each to ourselves that we are apt to live at random ? We are swayed by the circumstances which we ought to control. We find it a relief when we are spared (as we think) the necessity for reflection or decision : a book lightly taken up, a friend's visit, a fixed engagement, fill up the day with fragments ; and day follows day as a mere addition. There is no living idea to unite and harmonise the whole. Of course we cannot make, or to any great extent modify, the conditions under which we have to act ; but we can consciously render them tributary to one high purpose. We can regard them habitually in the light of our supreme end. This is, as it seems to me, the first result of zeal, and it is in spiritual matters as else-where, that great results are most surely gained by the accumulation of small things. If we strive con-tinuously towards a certain goal, the whole move-ment of our life, however slow, will be towards it, and as we move, the gathered force will make our progress more steady and more sure." [1]

To render every effort "tributary to one high purpose"—this was indeed the aim of Bishop West-cott's life ; to lead others to share in it was the object of all his teaching. At the beginning of a paper on Browning,[2] he has left us a picture of the true poet's work which might well stand also for his own.

"In my undergraduate days, if I remember rightly, I came across the description of a poet which speaks of him as one who 'sees the infinite in things.' The thought has been to me from that time forward a great help in studying the noblest poetry. The true poet does, I believe, of necessity see the infinite in his subject ; and he so presents his vision to his readers that they too, if their eyes are open, are enabled to share in its lessons."

Such was essentially his life-work ; and its far-reaching influence, and source of strength, also stand revealed by himself all unconsciously in his farewell tributes to the two friends most closely bound to him in work as well as in affection. Of Bishop Lightfoot he wrote :—

"The last secret of his strength, as it must be of our strength, was his devotion to a living God, as he worked from hour to hour 'face to face with the glory of the Eternal Father full upon him.'"[3]

While he summed up Dr. Hort's long labours in words that might have been written of his own :—

---

[1] *Steps in the Christian Life.*
[2] *Religions of the West*, p. 253.
[3] *From Strength to Strength.*

" A life so lived, however prolific in literary achievements, is more fruitful by what it is than by what it does." [1]

Towards the close of Bishop Westcott's last illness, we read in his *Life*, when his strength was failing, he asked for the day's Psalms to be read to him. " At first the Bishop tried to say the alternate verses, but this was more than he could do, so he listened, and joined in the Gloria. When this reading was finished, the Bishop, after thanking his daughters very lovingly, added, ' All I can do is a little bit of praise. Just a little bit of praise.' " [2]

They were almost the last words, the last effort of his life—" Just a little bit of praise."

[1] Preface to Dr. Hort's Hulsean Lectures on " The Way, the Truth, the Life."

[2] *Life of Bishop Westcott*.

II

GENERAL TEACHING

GENERAL TEACHING

"To sum up all then very briefly, the losing of self in the supreme thought of God is the secret of our power as Christians."—*Christian Life*.

"We shall be agreed, I assume, that the object of education is . . . to train the whole man for all life, for life seen and unseen, for the unseen through the seen and in the seen : to train citizens for the Kingdom of God. As we believe in God and the world to come, these must be master thoughts."—*Christian Aspects of Life*.

THEY were assuredly master thoughts with Bishop Westcott himself. Their dominating force grows more and more clear the more we study not his teaching only, but also its effect on other minds. In this we have, as I venture to think, the best commentary on the Bishop's writings. Judged by themselves they are, unquestionably, often difficult to follow, wanting in clearness, in definite expression, in practical application ; not the right books, therefore, we sometimes hear it said, for busy people needing practical help in daily life. And yet, what is actually the fact ? That library after library has the same report to give, of Bishop Westcott's being the theological works most constantly in request among busy workers no less than leisured students. While reader after reader has the same story to tell, of life grown nobler, and faith more real, in the light

of the unwearied viewing of all things in the light of
the presence and the glory of God.

From one comes the recognition of a new epoch
of spiritual life, dated from the reading of those
arresting glimpses of Francis of Assisi and George
Fox.[1]   Another can tell of the *meaning* of the
Resurrection brought home to his soul with a fresh
and living force by the *Revelation of the Risen
Lord*, and its more difficult companion, the *Gospel
of the Resurrection*.   While in yet another case,
the most casual observers recognise, though they
cannot understand, the gradual disciplining of effort
—the chastening of personal ambition into self-
surrender—to which the ardent worker has been
first encouraged, and then kept constant, by the
steadfast note of consecration echoed through all the
Bishop's writings.

Perhaps, if one looks a little deeper, the secret of
their power lies in this very fact, that their aim is so
clear and so unvarying, however different, or even
difficult, may be the forms in which it finds expression.   And that the great majority of those who are
not students, reading with heart rather than with
head, for the sake not so much of what they can
understand, as what they gain, do grasp those
central and pervading thoughts of God's glory and
man's consecration, untroubled by difficulties of
expression.

Perhaps these thoughts are set forth with the
greatest clearness in the sermons which Bishop
Westcott preached distinctively as an old man speaking to the young.

[1] In *Social Aspects of Christianity*.

" Our power of reverence is the measure of our power of rising.

" . . . Reverence is in all cases a true measure of our moral worth, and devotion a true measure of our strength." [1]

Such were the key-notes of his appeals to the rising generation to make a worthy use of their great gift of youth.

" Trust, then, I say, the noblest thoughts which God gives you, and translate them into action. . . . The vision of God is indeed the transfiguration of the world : communion with God is the inspiration of life. . . . If He is invisible, the blank is due to our blindness, and not to His absence." [1]

Thus it was that he addressed the boys of Sherborne, and his message to the Cambridge students was the same in substance, only clothed with deeper thoughts. One of his latest addresses to them bears the characteristic title, " Via Hominis, Visio Dei." [2] In this he says :—

" The way of man is the Vision of God. The Vision of God is the rule and the crown of life ; now through a glass in a riddle, as we strive to put together the lineaments of unearthly beauty dimly visible and only partially traced ; but then face to face, when we shall be transformed into that image which we were made to gain. We have the capacity for the vision, and God is pleased to satisfy it. . . .

[1] *Incarnation and Common Life* (" Sursum Corda ").
[2] *Christian Aspects of Life.*

C

". . . The Vision of God calls out all that is noblest in us, by revealing our affinity to our Father in Heaven, and imparts to him who has rested in its transforming light a power of bringing conviction to others, which none else can have. . . .

". . . The Vision of God brings a just proportion to our estimate of claims and actions, and makes clear that to love Him is the first commandment, and to seek His Kingdom the first duty. It guards us from the perils of living for the moment, and enables us to anticipate the verdict of righteous judgment. It lifts from us 'the weight of chance desires.' . . . The Vision of God calms the passion for excitement which masters and torments us as long as we forget His Majestic Presence. . . .

". . . *Via Hominis, Visio Dei.* No privilege can be greater than to direct one soul to that way of light which brightens to the perfect day, when there shall be night no more. No joy can be greater than to enter upon it, and to behold from afar the glory of the Lord, by which man is transformed into the same image, from glory to glory."

More personal still is the appeal in the sermon on the vision of Isaiah, preached in Cambridge on Trinity Sunday, 1885 [1] :—

". . . Brethren, if, as I believe, you have seen this, dimly, it may be, and but for a brief

[1] *Christus Consummator* ("The Vision of God the Call of the Prophet ").

moment; and you above all before whom the
work of life is opening with the fresh fulness of
promise in the purpose of God's grace,—be sure
that there is nothing in life more real than such
a vision. It is the pure light of heaven so
broken by the shadows of earth that we can
bear it. Do not then turn from it, or dismiss it
as a dream. It is easy, alas, to question the
authority of the greatest thoughts which God
sends to us. It is easy to darken them and to
lose them. But it is not easy to live on to the
end without them. . . . You must have been
allowed to feel that you are stirred with the
truest joy, and braced to labour best at your
little tasks, while you welcome and keep before
you the loftiest ideal of the method and the aim
of work and being which God has made known
to you. That is, indeed, His revelation, the
vision of Himself. So He declares what He
would have you to do, what He will enable you
to do. So He calls you to be prophets. . . .
The heart alone can speak to the heart. But
he who has beheld the least fragment of the
divine glory, he who has spelt out in letters of
light on the face of the world one syllable of the
Triune Name, will have a confidence and a
power which nothing else can bring. Only let
him trust what he has seen, and it will become
to him a guiding-star till he rests in the unveiled
presence of Christ. . . .

" . . . We shall say, with the lowliest confession of our unworthiness, ' our eyes have seen
the King, the Lord of Hosts.' "

This last address in *Christus Consummator*, thrilled as it is through and through with the expression as well as with the sense of awe, is a very good introduction to offer to those unfamiliar with Bishop Westcott's works. The earlier addresses in the book, on the Epistle to the Hebrews, are of course also full of interest, and the second, especially, comes home to all whose hearts have ached over the thought or the experience of suffering.

> "The virtue of the Lord's life made perfect through suffering guides us still. We know that not one day of His hidden discipline was fruitless. Each had its lesson of obedience; each marked a fresh advance in the consummation of manhood. So taught, we can feel how the lonely sufferer is still a fellow-worker with Him; how in the stillness of the night-watches a sleepless voice of intercession, unheard by man, but borne to God by a 'surrendered soul,' may bring strength to combatants wearied with a doubtful conflict; how the word 'one soweth and another reapeth,' may find a larger application than we have dreamed of, so that when we wake up we may be allowed to see that not one pang in the innumerable woes of men has been fruitless in purifying energy." [1]

This one endeavour, to look upon everything in life—love, joy, sorrow, labour, thought—as so many different veils through which to behold the glory of God, may be truly called the heart of Bishop

[1] *Christus Consummator*.

Westcott's teaching. Without this clearly before us, his books will remain obscure and puzzling to the last. Read in this light, they one and all repeat, in different forms and under different aspects, the one unwearied appeal of his whole life, *Sursum Corda*— Lift up your hearts! It was simply and solely *God* whom he set before those he taught : God, in all His unseen glory, as the one worthy end of all effort, hope, devotion ; to be sought in Sacraments, thought, and active service, all as acts of worship.

Lift up your hearts! It was most essentially the message of Bishop Westcott's own life that he sought with impassioned earnestness to pass on to those that should come after, and it rings across his grave with thrilling force. The power of that message, so delivered, is shown in the witness of lives purified, hearts touched and won, and world-wide fame gained without the seeking. The working of the power he has himself drawn for us in his picture of a life lived wholly in God's Presence.

" All that is required of the heavenward traveller . . . is perfect self-surrender and perfect trust. Yielding himself to the Spirit of God, the simplest believer will live with the power of a divine life. He will aim, not at some crown of privilege, but at showing the capacities of the common lot. . . . He will keep the vision of his ideal tranquil and pure, even when his efforts to reach it end in confusion and failure. . . . He will think nothing lost, because he offers all to God, who will guard what He receives. He will think nothing impossible, because God, in His own good time, will fulfil the thought which He inspires." [1]

Such was the Bishop's vision of the Christian life; and for those who might challenge it as impossible to realise, he had an answer.

"As the vision rises before us . . . we cry again, bowed down by past failures, '*Who is sufficient for these things?*' There can be but one answer—he who wholly forgets himself in God who called him; he who 'lays down at the footstool of God his successes and his failures, his hopes and his fears, his knowledge and his ignorance, his weakness and his strength, his misgivings and his confidence — all that he is and all that he might be—content to take up thence just that which God shall give him.'" [2]

For a prayer for strength to reach this high ideal —for faith to keep this vision of God ever before our eyes—we may well turn to the Bishop's own Collect for the purpose :—

"O Lord God, in whom we live and move and have our being, Open our eyes that we may behold Thy Fatherly Presence ever about us. Draw our hearts to Thee with the power of Thy love. Teach us to be careful for nothing; and when we have done what Thou hast given us to do, help us, O God our Saviour, to leave the issue to Thy wisdom. Take from us all doubt

[1] *From Strength to Strength.*   [2] *Ibid.*

and distrust. Lift our thoughts up to Thee
in heaven ; and make us to know that all things
are possible to us through Thy Son, our Re-
deemer.   Amen." [1]

[1] *Common Prayers for Family Use.*

III

FOUNDATION TRUTHS

FOUNDATION TRUTHS

" The Faith in the Resurrection can harmonise life : can inspire life : can transform life."—*Christian Life, Manifold and One.*

" We look round and find no help adequate to our needs. We do not—this is the secret of every failure—believe in the Holy Ghost. . . . He is, we profess, ' the Lord, the Giver of Life ' ; and He is this, not in some remote sphere, but here and now. Do we then, from day to day, in our work and in our rest, look to Him, offer ourselves to Him, listen for His voice, withdraw nothing from His purifying influence, and confide in complete self-surrender upon His unfailing grace."—*Incarnation and Common Life.*

" A theory of the Atonement may be a minister of faith, but the fact of the Atonement is the inspiration of faith."—*Victory of the Cross.*

BISHOP WESTCOTT'S teaching has been called " indefinite " by those who do not enter into it. The criticism is simply mistaken in so far as it suggests any uncertainty in his own grasp of the truths he taught ; that he did not attempt to define their outlines is the fact. His endeavour was rather to make clear their inmost meaning. He never could forget that in defining a truth we also limit it.

" All formulas are of the nature of outlines," he wrote. " They define by exclusion as well as by comprehension." And he was fond of quoting the saying of a great artist—" There is no outline in nature."

Definitions of great truths have, of course, their

very great use ; only, as we have no lack of teachers to draw them for us, we need not regret that Bishop Westcott devoted his great powers to pointing out the glory rather than the limits of the faith in which he lived.

Not that he regarded Christian doctrine as in any sense unnecessary ; on the contrary, he looked upon it, with his unvarying singleness of vision, as a practical means of bringing men's minds into closer touch with God.

" Christian doctrine "—so he taught—" is designed to direct and sustain us in our efforts to hold a personal and living intercourse with a personal and living Lord." [1]

[1] *Christian Aspects.*

i. The Incarnation and Resurrection

Two doctrines above all others are dwelt upon throughout Bishop Westcott's writings as the foundation of all true life—the Incarnation and the Resurrection of our Lord Jesus Christ. To the Bishop these were not merely theological phrases, but the spring and the power of every effort. "The Incarnation a Revelation of Human Duties" is the title of the charge to his clergy which dealt the most directly with practical problems.[1] His aim in this was to show that "we have in the fact of the Incarnation, which it is our duty to proclaim, a motive adequate to stir us to resolute action, and strength adequate to support us in the face of difficulties apparently insuperable : that the vision of the patience of God is able to bring back confidence when we are disheartened by disappointments and delays . . . that the Incarnation of the Word of God becomes to us, as we meditate on the fact, a growing revelation of duties personal, social, national. . . ."

The power of the Incarnation as a practical help in daily life to those who " meditate on the fact "— that was the thought chiefly insisted on ; and with it

[1] In *The Incarnation and Common Life.*

was joined an earnest appeal for the recognition of that power in every sphere of thought and action. "We are bound not only to believe that 'Jesus is Lord,' but to confess Him before men."

"For if the message of the Incarnation necessarily transcends our thoughts in its fulness, none the less it comes within the range of our experience as far as our thoughts can reach. It touches life at every point, and we are bound to consider what it means for us, for our fellow-men, and for the world. It is not enough to hold it as an article of our creed : we must openly and in secret prove its efficacy in action. By our reticence, by our habitual reserve in dealing with it as the master-power in shaping and sustaining our thoughts, our purposes, our deeds, we encourage a feeling of secret mistrust as to the validity of the Faith."

"The master-power in shaping and sustaining our thoughts, our purposes, our deeds" : this, and nothing less, is what we are bidden to find in the fact that in our Lord Jesus Christ, God became man, and man was made one with God. The Bishop was never weary of calling upon those whom he taught, to strive to enter more fully into the meaning of St. Paul's favourite phrase "*in Christ.*" In these two words he held that we have both the mystery and the power of the Incarnation summed up. The thought is so tremendous, and the phrase so familiar, that we are sometimes apt to miss the fulness of its meaning.

In Christ : those for whom the words have as yet

but little force, may gain new and undreamed-of light from the three first addresses in *Christian Aspects of Life*, in which the Bishop dwells upon the phrase again and again to try and suggest ever-fresh depths of teaching.

" Those who are *in Christ* "—he says, in words that unconsciously sum up his own life—" are bound to serve God with their whole being ; with their intellect no less than with their heart and their strength and their substance. They are distinguished from others, not by any difference in the strenuousness of their labours, but by their motive and their aim. For them all that falls within human observation is a potential parable of spiritual realities, through which a fresh vision may be gained of the glory of God. They will be the keenest of men to watch for the dawn of new ideas. For them there can be no despond-ency and no indifference. They bring to the Lord the first-fruits of all that He has lent to them, and commit their gains to His keeping." (P. 32.)

". . . Nor is it without significance that the dominant phrase in St. Paul is 'we in Christ,' and not 'Christ in us.' He is in us, as we are in Him. But the use of the phrase 'in Christ' takes us at once to the spiritual realm, and fixes our thoughts on the centre of unity, the one common Divine fountain of life. . . . In Christ we do not 'press on to perfection,' but are 'borne to it,' as we yield ourselves to His vital influence. . . .

" . . . *In Christ* fixes our attention on the will of God, and not on our own powers or achievements. It enables us in all delays to *win our souls in patience*. It quickens our eyes to see the eternal in every common thing about us. It opens our ears to the many voices of the Holy Spirit, who is even now taking of the things of Christ and revealing them to us." (P. 19.)

" In Him we live, and in Him we have through His human nature and His earthly life a perfect revelation of the Father. . . ." (P. 28.)

" . . . This thought of man's divine sonship in the Son of Man . . . throws light on the Communion of Saints. Whoever is in Christ, is in fellowship with all who are in Him. In Him we are in fellowship with the dead in Christ. Whatever ministry we are allowed to offer to the least member of His Body in prayer or service reaches to them ; and, though the veil is not lifted from the unseen world, we may believe that whatever ministry they render reaches to us also in blessing through the unity of the one life." (P. 34.)

" . . . So far as we are *in Christ*, we cannot fail to hear His living voice." (P. 52.)

In the same way Bishop Westcott strove to bring the meaning of the Resurrection home to the souls of those to whom he ministered. The Incarnation was to him the consecration of life ; the Resurrection was its strength. In the fact that God had become man, he found hope for the hallowing of man's nature ; in the fact that God, as man, had proved stronger than death, and had revealed Himself in the unchanged personality of His Risen Life, he found the power by which that hope could be fulfilled.

No matter what were the subjects with which he dealt, these two thoughts were always present, whether or no they were definitely expressed. God had become one with mankind in Christ; therefore in Christ also mankind had power to become one with God. Christ after His Resurrection had shown Himself in personal relations with men; therefore death had no longer power to interpose a barrier— men throughout all ages could continue in personal relations with Him, and find in Him their Friend, their Strength, their Life.

" A Christian "—the Bishop wrote in his *Gospel of the Resurrection*—" is one who throws himself with absolute confidence upon a living Lord."

It was of the *Gospel of the Resurrection* that he wrote: " It is the only one of my books that I care much about, and I hope it will do some good." The hope has been abundantly fulfilled in many a soul that has learned from it to look upon the Resurrection as " not an isolated fact, but emphatically a revelation," through which we can discern the personal and unchanging power and presence of our Lord Jesus Christ.

" We are not Christians "—the Bishop insists in the introduction—" unless we are clear in our confession on this point. To preach the fact of Resurrection was the first function of the Evangelists; to embody the doctrine of the Resurrection is the great office of the Church; to learn the meaning of the Resurrection is the task not of one age only, but of all." (P. 8.)

To make this meaning clear is the whole purpose of this book that was so near his heart ; and he does so by dealing with the Resurrection first as a historical fact, and afterwards as the revelation through which we gain new views of nature, of history, of humanity, and of the Church.

" It is my object "—he explains at the opening —" to show that a belief in the Resurrection of our Lord is not indeed the solution (for that we cannot gain), but the illumination of the mysteries of life : that in this fact the apparent contradictions of the immensity and insignificance of the individual are harmonised : that in this lies an end to which pre-Christian history converged, a spring from which post-Christian history flows : that in this man finds the only perfect consecration of his entire nature." (P. 3.)

On the first and vital necessity of recognising the Resurrection as a historical fact, he was very urgent.

" According to the divine instinct of the first age, the message of the Resurrection sums up in one fact the teaching of the Gospel. It is the one central link between the seen and the unseen. We cannot allow our thoughts to be vague or undecided upon it with impunity. We must place it in the very front of our confession, with all that it includes, or we must be prepared to lay aside the Christian name." (P. 7.)

" . . . The Resurrection, then, is either a fact

in itself wholly independent of those who were witnesses to it, or it is a fiction—it matters not whether designed or undesigned—on which no belief can be founded. It is a real link between the seen and the unseen worlds, or it is at best the expression of a human instinct. . . . A splendid guess, an inextinguishable desire, alone have sought to pierce the darkness beyond the tomb, if Jesus has not (as we believe) borne our human nature into the presence of God." (P. 5.)

" . . . The Death, the Burial, and the Resurrection of Christ, claim to be facts exactly in the same sense, to be supported by evidence essentially identical in kind, and to be bound together indissolubly as the groundwork of the Christian Faith. If they are true, then they will be seen to form the centre round which other truths group themselves, not less real, nor less significant, though they are not equally capable of being directly subjected to historical tests. If they are not true, then 'is our faith vain.'" (P. 3.)

This was the alternative that Bishop Westcott placed before his readers in no uncertain manner. Either the Resurrection must be accepted as a fact of history, or the title of Christian must be abandoned as an empty name.

The *meaning* of the fact has next to be considered —that anxious question which has echoed in so many minds, as to what difference it makes to ourselves personally to believe that our Lord Jesus Christ did actually rise again from the dead. The Bishop has answered this by showing, with the force of intense conviction, what the Resurrection has meant, first to the Apostles, and through them to all who believe.

"The ground on which the Apostles rested their appeal was the Resurrection; the function which they claimed for themselves was to bear witness to it. Their belief was not an idle assent, but the spring of a new life.

"Those who, when Christ was yet with them, wavered in spite of their love for Him, mistook His words, misunderstood His purpose, forsook Him at His Passion, after a brief interval court danger in the service of a Master no longer present, proclaim with unfaltering zeal a message hitherto unheard, build up a society in faith on His Name, extend to Samaritans and Gentiles the blessings which were promised to the people of God. However we explain it, the change is complete and certain. Their whole moral nature was transformed." (P. 120.)

The effects of the Resurrection on the Lord's immediate disciples are dealt with at length in the sections from which these passages are taken. The effects, through the Apostles, upon all believers, are splendidly summed up at the end of the book, and are shown more fully in the companion volume, *The Revelation of the Risen Lord.*

"The Resurrection of Christ is no isolated fact. It is not only an answer to the craving of the human heart; it is the key to all history, the interpretation of the growing purpose of life." (P. 55.)

" . . . Every energy will be turned to its proper

work as our thoughts rest on the glory of the Risen Saviour." (P. 246.) [1]

The arguments showing the transforming power of this one supreme fact of the Resurrection on our views alike of history, nature, humanity, and the Church of Christ, must be studied in detail to be understood. The closeness of their reasoning makes them not always easy to follow, except by an accustomed reader, so that it will often be found a good plan to begin with the simpler *Revelation of the Risen Lord*. It was written to illustrate the *Gospel of the Resurrection*, and excellently it serves the purpose. The shorter chapters into which it is divided make it far easier reading, and the teaching throughout is intensely personal. The different appearances of the Risen Saviour are described with a beauty and vividness that appeal to every reader, and make clear the personal meaning for all Christians which lies behind the outward revelations through love and thought, and labour, and patient waiting, and even doubt itself when truly faced.

" The Lord appears to one and to many : to the loving, the waiting, the desponding, the doubtful : in the garden, on the way, in the room, on the shore, on the hillside. Now He is recognised at once, now slowly and with growing conviction. But with every variety of circumstance there is one effect. The natural impression is—not to go further now—that the revelation was given according to the need and the power

[1] *Revelation of the Risen Lord.*

of those who received it : and hence we are encouraged to conclude that by this means the record corresponds with the needs and powers of all Christians to the end of time. As the revelation was a discipline and preparation then, so the record is a discipline and preparation now. The record is fragmentary, but it is also divinely typical. That which is incomplete as a history is complete as a Gospel." (P. 6.)

" . . . If we now turn to the Revelation itself, two characteristics will at once strike us. It is a revelation of new modes of human life : it is a revelation made only to believers. It is not the exhibition of the continuance of an existence with which we are already acquainted, but the indication of an existence for which we look. It is for the Church and not for the world, to strengthen not to overpower. The Revelation of the Risen Christ is indeed, in the fullest sense of the word, a Revelation—an unveiling of that which was before undiscovered and unknown." (P. 7.)

" . . . The substance of faith is not a fact which we cannot explain away, or a conclusion which we cannot escape, but the personal apprehension of a living, loving Friend. And Christ still makes Himself known in His Church and in each believer's heart by words of peace. He is still with us the same as eighteen hundred years ago, unchanged and unchangeable, the same yesterday, to-day, and for ever." (P. 102.)

" . . .. Under one aspect then, Christ, the Risen Christ, is everywhere present though our eyes be

holden, and in Him all things are ; but this
history of the journey to Emmaus carries with it
other and more personal teachings. It brings
before us how Christ, the Risen Christ, in a
special sense draws near to each one of us severally : how He adds Himself to the two or three
gathered together in His name : how He journeys
with us : how He enlightens our reason and fires
our affections : how at some supreme moment,
it may be, He allows us to see, with the eyes of
the spirit, a brief vision of His majesty. For
that which was enacted on the evening of the
first Lord's Day has been fulfilled, and is fulfilled
no less surely and tenderly through the experience of all believers. Christ draws near to
us now, as to those unknown wayfarers, with
purposes of love. Christ draws near to us when
in the sacred intercourse of friendship we speak
of our highest hopes and of our greatest sorrows,
when we dare to throw off the veil of conventional
irony, and talk openly of that which we know to
lie deepest in our nature. Christ draws near us
at the sad season when He seems to have been
finally taken away, if we are not ashamed to
confess, in the apparent disappointment of our
hopes, that we are still His disciples." (P. 52.)

Such are the general lines of the Bishop's teaching on the Resurrection as a practical power in daily
life. Those who study that teaching for the first
time will be amazed at the new light it brings. It
is more than an advance—a transformation, rather
—in the Christian life, when the soul first gains a

glimpse into the *personal* meaning of the Resurrection, not merely as a fact to be accepted as true, but as the power which can glorify all life and love and effort, in the perpetual Presence of a living Lord.

Each one must realise that Presence for himself; only in Bishop Westcott's writings we are brought into touch with one who beyond all manner of doubt had found it, and with it rest, and strength, and joy. And this conviction has inspired many an anxious seeker with fresh courage in the quest.

2. The Work of the Holy Spirit

"Do we believe in the Holy Ghost? If we believe, all things are possible to us; if we do not believe, then for us Christ is not risen."[1]

Thus Bishop Westcott links together, in their practical results upon the life of Christians, the doctrines of the Resurrection of Christ, and of the mission of the Holy Spirit. He always looked upon this less as a new beginning than as the consequence and completion of all that had gone before.

"By His Life and Death and Resurrection and Ascension, the Incarnate Son revealed God as Father, and taught us what the Father is—His Father and our Father—in the sovereignty of His infinite power, in the righteousness of His infinite wisdom, in the tenderness of His infinite love. He brought home to us the truth of Divine Fatherhood in the terms of human knowledge, and taught each man to say, looking to Heaven with a new confidence, not 'our Father' only, but 'Father,' 'my Father.'"[2]

The words come from the Bishop's address on

[1] *Christian Aspects*, p. 117.
[2] *Incarnation and Common Life*, p. 110.

41

" The Spirit sent in the Name of the Son," the
title of which is characteristic of his teaching.   To
him the Holy Spirit was essentially the " Spirit of
Jesus," and the strength of his life lay in realising,
as he himself said, " His unseen Presence through
the Spirit."   With his deep insight he discerned
the fatal results of the false spirituality, the vain
confidence, and the unchastened devotion, which
arise from any separation between the thought of the
Holy Spirit and the thought of Christ ; and in this
same address he sought to make the danger clear.

" To him that believeth all things are possible.
But to make this possibility a fact, we need, and
we all know sadly that we need, the fresh
conviction of a Spiritual Presence in our troubled
world, and spiritual fellowship with the unseen
realised through the fulness of our humanity.
Many seek it in strange, unhallowed ways, and
all the while the blessing is offered to us by the
Spirit sent in Christ's name, who is disclosing to
souls opened to Him fresh mysteries of the
Incarnation." [1]

To Bishop Westcott the thought of Pentecost did
not mean, as with so many teachers, merely a new
beginning, but rather the completion and fulfilment
of all that had gone before.   This thought is made
specially clear in Lecture VIII. of the *Historic Faith*,
perhaps the fullest expression among his writings of
his teaching on the Holy Spirit.

" At the Incarnation, the Baptism, the Tempta-

[1] *Incarnation and Common Life*, p. 121.

tion, the Spirit who was active at the creation of man was revealed as active at his new creation. But it was not till the full consequences of sin had been borne, and death had been conquered, and humanity had been raised in the Son of Man to the right hand of God, that the rushing wind and fiery tongues told outwardly, at the festival of the gathered harvest, of the promise of the Father." (P. 45.)

"The festival of the gathered harvest"— the phrase fills the thought of Pentecost with a depth of meaning that grows in splendour as we ponder it.

The whole of this lecture will repay the most careful study, full as it is of thoughts for all. The power of the Holy Spirit *for all*—as "bringing home Christ and the things of Christ to each man and to all men"—that was what Bishop Westcott strove to teach. All the weakness, all the weariness, all the faint-hearted failures of life, he saw as the dulness of vision by which "we forget that the seal of the Spirit is on our foreheads, and that we have only to claim our heritage and go forth to share in a victory which has been already won."

"*I believe in the Holy Ghost.* He who is able to make the confession has found a divine Friend. For him the Spirit is not an influence, an energy, of One far off, but a present Comforter whom Christ has sent to fulfil His work, a present Guide ready to lead him into all the Truth, a present Advocate waiting to gain acceptance for the deep sighings of the heart

before the throne of God.   So it is that Scripture
speaks of His relation to us: so it is that we
can understand how His Presence among men is
dependent on the exaltation of Christ in His
human nature to the right hand of God.

"*I believe in the Holy Ghost.*   He who is able
to make the confession recognises the action of
One who is moulding his single life.   Each
believer is himself a temple to be prepared for
the Master's dwelling.   The same Spirit who
shapes the course of the whole world, hallows
the soul which is offered to Him for a divine
use.   The Christian believer is in one sense
alone with God, and God alone with him.   He
has a work to do—definite, individual, eternal,
through the ordinary duties and occupations and
trials of common business ; and this the Spirit
sent in Christ's name, bringing to him the virtue
of Christ's humanity, will help him to perfect.

"*I believe in the Holy Ghost.*   Life is indeed
full of mysteries to which we can give no
interpretation, of griefs to which we can gain no
present remedy.   I have no will to extenuate
them.   Nay, rather we must feel them deeply if
we are to know God ; and then the faith in the
personal help of the Holy Spirit—the comple-
ment of the Incarnation—is sufficient for our
needs.

"The prayer of the warrior of old time be-
wildered by the darkness was : 'Give light and
let me die.'   We can say : 'Help us to live,
and the light will come'— come through life
itself.

" So may we cherish each impulse towards good as the direct inspiration of God, which bears with it the assurance of its accomplishment. So may we watch the signs of an unseen power moulding us by gentlest influences to the pattern of a divine likeness. So may we have our eyes opened to see a heavenly order slowly fulfilled about us. In that conviction, in that experience, in that vision, we shall work on with the certain knowledge that each effort is blessed by Him who inspired it. Each age, each heart, has its own questionings, but Christ's words are addressed to every age and to every heart : they can never want their accomplishment : *The Paraclete, even the Holy Spirit, whom the Father will send in My name, He shall teach you all things.*" [1]

[1] *The Historic Faith*, Lect. VIII.

3. THE ATONEMENT

OF all the truths which form the foundation of our faith, the doctrine of the Atonement is perhaps the one most commonly neglected. Chiefly, it may be, because the meaning of it is hard to grasp, and so many Christians persuade themselves that what is difficult is also unnecessary. Here again Bishop Westcott's teaching comes to our help, showing us what the doctrine of the Atonement, wrought by our Lord Jesus Christ, means for each one of us, as a *fact* of the closest personal importance in every individual life.

This was the point on which he laid especial stress. As he wrote to a friend :

" . . . There has never been any authoritative *theory* of the Atonement laid down in our Church, or in any of the historic churches. The *fact* that Christ died for our sins and for the whole world is firmly held, and we endeavour to see what light this fact throws upon our own state, and our relations to God and man. That is all." [1]

The Bishop's own teaching on the subject is, of course, very fully given in his *Commentary on the Gospel of St. John*. It is more briefly and simply

[1] *Life of Bishop Westcott*, vol. ii. p. 220.

expressed in the series of addresses contained in his *Victory of the Cross*, of which he said, in the letter above quoted :

> " I do not think that I ever took more pains on anything than on the lectures on the subject which I gave at Hereford Cathedral. No doubt many do not agree with me, but I do not think that any one would say that the view which I maintain is opposed to anything in our formularies."

In these addresses are traced out, step by step, the successive thoughts by which the *meaning* of the Atonement may be most clearly grasped by the individual soul. The purpose of the book is that " some may find even in this sketch fresh gladness and strength, through the conviction which I have sought to convey, that the Victory of the Cross is revealed to us with fresh glory by thoughts which are characteristic of our own age." I have thought that to try and give some idea of these thoughts, in their own order, may be the best way of attracting readers to a closer study of them in the book itself.

1. *The Natural Fellowship of Man*

This is the thought to which Bishop Westcott first points us, as the root of the whole matter. He bids us consider our necessary dependence one upon another, and each upon all, in every department of life ; work, teaching, sustenance, joy and sorrow, achievement and also failure, disease and sin. It is only what we all know before, as he points out ;

but he would have us hold the thought more closely, and take account of what it means to us in our spiritual lives.

> " In this intimate, indestructible fellowship, Nature . . . shows us the possibility of a Redemption, and she also shows us the condition. The possibility lies in our fellowship : the condition is fixed in sacrifice." (Pp. 21, 22.)

2. *Sacrifice as the Highest Power in Life*

This is the next thought to which we are led on.

> " Looking away then from the Gospel for a moment, I venture to say that the voice of humanity itself declares, as the lesson of the ages, that sacrifice alone is fruitful." (P. 23.)

And this lesson is taught through that very sense of fellowship first insisted on.

> " The essence of sin is selfishness in respect of men, and self-assertion in respect of God ; the unloving claim of independence, the arrogant isolation of our interests. . . . We live through others. The sacrifice and suffering of others minister to us from the cradle to the grave. And in turn we serve our fellows, knowing the destination of our labours or not knowing it, willingly, or even against our will. Vicarious toil, pain, suffering, is the very warp of life. When the divine light falls upon it, it becomes transformed into sacrifice. . . ." (P. 24.)

The life lived to itself, and by itself, is bound to perish ; the life given for others—whether in labour, pain, or death—lives on in them, and by their added strength. And this power of sacrifice, we are shown, " is of universal range." It was recognised by noble spirits before Christ came into the world ; it is offered to us in every region of our lives.

" The call to sacrifice, with the trial and crown, the crown of self-surrender, comes to us in many forms. But it does come to all with the same richness of benediction. It comes to us by our own fireside, and it comes to us in business and in society. It comes to husband and wife, to parents and children, to teacher and scholar, to friends, to fellow-workmen. We can all obey it, and for the most part we can all evade it. But in each case we know that it has come, and that it has left its trace behind. We are not afterwards what we were before we either welcomed or refused the opportunity for self-denial. We are stronger or weaker. Our sympathies are broader or narrower. Our spiritual vision is keener or duller. Life is for us larger in meaning or promise, or brought more near to the standard of our self-chosen littleness.

" . . . All this is the teaching of nature on sacrifice, stern in the sure sentence of retribution as it is fertile in general inspiration." (P. 34.)

E

3. *The Unity of Humanity in Christ*

From the teaching of humanity we pass on to the revelation of the Gospel. We are shown how in Christ Jesus—perfect God and perfect Man—the natural fellowship of humanity "is raised to a divine unity, so that the possibility of Redemption is made a fact."

The possibility of Redemption is made a fact—that is the tremendous thought which has next to be pondered. And ´the very difficulty we find in making it our own points us to the importance of grasping the full meaning of *every* article of our Baptismal Creed ; of the articles dealing with the Birth of our Lord, no less than those on His Death and Resurrection. We are shown, in a splendid passage (p. 44), that in proportion as we truly realise the meaning of the Incarnation, can we enter also into the thought of the absolute union of Christ with the members of "the Church which is His body"—a union so complete that they are in very deed *in Him*, with all their weakness, and He *in them*, with all His strength.

The very immensity of the thought makes it impossible even to suggest in any brief outline ; each one must needs make it his own by study, and effort, and often suffering. Perhaps the utmost that one mind can do for another is so to suggest the splendour of the thought, and its personal value to each individual soul, as to kindle the desire for a deeper understanding, to pursue it further. And this is exactly what Bishop Westcott has done for his readers. He sets before them this thought of human fellowship raised *in Christ* to divine unity as the secret of life's highest powers, and, therefore, well worth taking pains to make our own.

"This is the common thought which can hallow every effort, which can nerve us for concentrated labour, which can bear us beyond the narrow limits of personal aims, which can bind together with the strength of their manifold energies the scholar and the artist, and the trader and the craftsman. 'We are Christians.' By that confession we know the vastness, the fulness, the unity of life *in Christ*.

"*Ye are all one man in Christ Jesus.* As we ponder the words and follow them beyond this region of conflict and succession, they disclose a prospect in which our souls can rest. The light of eternity falls for a space upon this changing world, that we may take heart in all that we count failure. . . . We are no longer independent, scattered units, but all in Him. The many are one. The glory of the whole is the joy of all, one joy in one life.

"Words fail; thought fails; but the Body of Christ and the Spirit of God fail not. Touched by the vision, we come back to our common daily work. Distracted, baffled, wearied, we have found the fulness of life complete in spite of our divisions; the promise of life sure in spite of our failures; the motive of life prevailing over all selfishness; when we hear the voice of God, *Ye are all one man in Christ Jesus*." (Pp. 53, 54.)

Thus Bishop Westcott sums up the glory of this thought of life *in Christ* and its power ; while the way of making it our own is suggested in a few words that repay long pondering.

"The law of material life corresponds with the law of spiritual life. Our natural life is represented by the appropriation and use of energy which is accessible to us. Our spiritual life is the appropriation and use of Him who is *the Life*. Our material food becomes for us the force through which the generous deed, the stirring speech, the lofty thought, is possible. The bread of life becomes for us the force through which, according to our faith, we realise the life of God in order that we may *glorify our Father which is in Heaven*." (P. 49.)

4. *The Sufferings of Christ*

This thought of human fellowship raised to unity *in Christ* is the beginning of the whole doctrine of the Atonement, but it is not the end. From it we are led on to consider the *sufferings of Christ* as the means by which that unity has been accomplished. In these sufferings we are shown not only the measure of divine love and human sin, but also the power of obedience as the only force by which God's love and strength and healing can be brought within reach of sinful man.

"Christ died, not to show His love by dying, but to give life to the world. *Therefore*, He says, *does the Father love Me, because I lay down*

My life, that I may take it again. That I may
take it again—death was in this case not only
faithfully borne, but rightly chosen, because in
the actual state of men it was the only way
through which the Son of Man could bring
humanity to life." (P. 70.)

And this thought of Christ's sufferings sheds new
light also on whatever we ourselves are called upon
to suffer. This is what we have next to realise.

"What then shall we say of suffering? Oh,
my friends, do we not feel that when we know
that we are children of God, such a question is
irrelevant? Shall we not leave all to the loving
wisdom of our Father. His will has become our
will: His end our end. If it be seen that the way
for us lies through purifying, bracing chastise-
ments, here or hereafter, can we desire that one
should be withheld? We look not only for redemption but for consummation in Christ. Our
cleansing is that we may be enabled to draw
near to God in worship, and at last through His
hallowing grace attain to His likeness. The joy
of such a destiny will transform every pain
through which it is approached. . . . We have
no promise that we shall be free from suffering :
it is enough that no suffering shall be fruitless
which is seen in the issue of the Father's will."
(P. 88.)

5. *The Virtue of Christ's Sacrifice*

The actual meaning of that sacrifice to ourselves, as a living, personal power to strengthen and transform our very being—this is the thought which we next reach.   And here again the very vastness of the thought will crush our efforts to grasp it, if it be not used to stimulate them.   A careless and superficial study of such a subject is worse than useless ; it is an actual hindrance.   Here, if anywhere, " every thought and every word must be guarded from the suspicion of presumption, and laid in the light of Christ."

"And however carefully we may strive to make the virtue of Christ's sacrifice more intelligible to ourselves, we must remember that the reality of its virtue is that by which we live."

For—and this sentence should be graven on the heart of every one who approaches the subject—

"*A theory of the Atonement may be a minister of faith, but the fact of the Atonement is the inspiration of faith.*"

For every one among us—learned and unlearned all alike—the matter of first importance is not to define or explain the Atonement, but to live by its power.   Bishop Westcott would have us take warning by the confusions of thought that have already arisen through false or narrow definitions.

"It is easier, indeed, to present in a definite shape systems of human reasoning than a view of the ways of God. . . . We are tempted to use temporal measures for the eternal : to judge

of the unseen by the material : to forget that
sinfulness is indeed the punishment of sin : . . .
to regard chastisement as the expression of
anger, and not as the tender discipline of
wisdom. . . . Thus we are tempted ; and we
carry even unconsciously our own materialising
fancies into the language of the Lord and His
Apostles. Where they speak of sin we substitute punishment. They represent evil as a
barrier which hinders the outflow of divine love
upon the guilty : we think of it as that which
entails painful retribution. They concentrate our
faith upon the assurance of a restored harmony
with God : we lower this transfiguring hope to
the removal of consequences which can be expressed in terms of earthly experience." (Pp.
77, 78.)

Four thoughts the Bishop offers, to help us to
realise the *power* of Christ's sufferings as a practical
force in our lives :—

" 1. Christ exhausted all suffering, bearing it
according to the will and mind of God.

2. We on our part need the constant support of
His present sympathy in our labours.

3. Christ is able to communicate the virtue of
His work, the reality of forgiveness, to all
who are in Him.

4. We on our part can even now, through every
trial, realise His joy." (P. 80.)

As we ponder these thoughts, we shall surely
find that " the example of His Life is filled with a
new energy."

"He does not leave us desolate. And in Him is the divine love visible. It is a fearful thing to fall into the hands of the living God; but, as it has been truly said, 'the hands of the living God' are what we call 'the laws of Nature.' What then if we come to know them as 'the everlasting arms,' the laws of the Divine Father-hood, to which we must desire to commit our-selves?" (P. 84.)

The vision is a glorious one; and from the thought of the life of God in Christ, shown in support and strength, we pass on naturally to its final and highest expression, in forgiveness. On that deepest of mysteries and most personal of needs, which we all have to consider in relation either to ourselves or to others, the following passage is full of suggestion:

"True forgiveness is indeed the energy of love answered by love. The forgiveness which remits a punishment may leave the heart untouched. The forgiveness which remits a sin includes by its very nature the return of responsive gratitude. The believer makes Christ's work his own, and God sees in him the Son of man." (P. 85.)

The importance of realising this, the true view of the Atonement, has to be brought home to the soul.

"We must jealously guard this truth of the transforming power of union with Christ. No parody of evangelical teaching can be more false than that which represents it as the discharge of the sinful, being sinful still, from the penalty of their guilt, by the intervention of the guiltless. *There can be no discharge of the sinful while they keep their sin.*" (P. 87.)

And then, yet once again, we come back to the root of the whole matter :

"The virtue of Christ's sacrifice is not a vain thing for us : it is our life." (P. 92.)

6. *Christ reigning from the Cross*

This is the last and crowning aspect under which to view the work of the Atonement. We need to contemplate the Lord Jesus as not only our Saviour, but our King. In the vision of Christ reigning from the Cross we see a sovereignty at once new, universal, present, and divine.

New, because it was won by suffering and obedience, not by self-assertion and might.

Universal, because it claims all, and appeals to all. " It claims, with the attractiveness of blessing, the service of every man. It leaves none desolate or uncared for, or unoccupied." (P. 98.)

Present, "because it is not for some distant future only, when there shall be no more sorrow and no more sin. It is for the transformation of the world which He has conquered. . . . It is directed to bring our common impulses under the conscious rule of a will harmonious with the will of God." (Pp. 98, 99.)

Divine, because " it answers to the very nature of God. God is love, and in love He reveals Himself as King. . . . Mere dogma in itself is powerless to stir the heart ; but when it is seen in a Person, the soul feels its influence. Devotion flows from the joyful sense of dependence on a living Lord. *We love Him because He first loved us.*" (P. 100.)

Thoughts such as these are not easy to master, but they are of intense and untold value. In themselves they are, as Bishop Westcott claims, in his concluding summary of the subject, " not so much difficult as strange."

> " They are not for students and scholars only, but for every believer who looks directly to Christ. They reach to the inmost depths of our common life. . . . There is in the soul that which leaps up in quick response to the greatest hope. . . . If we are mean and narrow and unloving, we shall be beggars in the midst of luxury, and desolate among a multitude of flatterers. If we behold God, if we behold Christ reigning from the Cross, suffering will be made the fuel of a purer joy." (P. 108.)

For " CHRIST, THE LIVING CHRIST, REIGNS FROM THE CROSS WITH A DOMINION WHICH KNOWS NO BOUNDS."

IV

BIBLE STUDY

BIBLE STUDY

*"In every variety of circumstance, in times of doubt and contro-
versy, in the face of new problems, in the interpretation of old formulæ,
I have found in the study of Holy Scripture unfailing strength and
light, limited only by my own infirmities."—Lessons from Work.*

"UNFAILING strength and light"—they are so
entirely the blessings which we are all taught to
seek in our Bible study, and which we so often fail
to find there, that we turn with eagerness to any
teacher who can tell us how they are to be gained.
And the first question with which we test his teaching is, how far it answers to our own personal and
practical needs.

This, and this only, is the question by which I
have tried to analyse Bishop Westcott's teaching on
the subject. Upon his profound and brilliant learning I have not presumed to touch. It is known
and respected by all who are qualified to appreciate
it, and this book is not for them. Through the
kindness of the Rev. Arthur Westcott, I am able to
add a chapter dealing with the larger works which
have fixed Dr. Westcott's high place in the world of
scholars.[1] But for the rest, my aim has been to
show not the intellectual so much as the practical

[1] See p. 201.

value which his writings have also for that large
class of readers who, like myself, can lay no claim
to scholarship.

For the sake of clearness, I have divided the
subject under three heads, according to the aspects
in which, as it seems to me, the Bishop most characteristically viewed the problems of Bible study in
his endeavours to help other minds.　They are the
points also which press most closely home upon all
who try to practise that study with any earnestness :
the difficulties to be faced ; the way in which the
Bible should be looked upon, as a whole ; and how
to study it in detail.

One caution I would add, to prevent the disappointment of those who are led to look in a book
for what they do not find.

The true value of Bishop Westcott's teaching
cannot be gained from a brief outline, or a few
striking sentences.　These only serve to direct the
reader to the rich stores of helpful thought—helpful,
as I believe, to *all* who will take pains to master it
—to be found by the patient and earnest study of
the Bishop's writings.　As he himself insisted, in
words which deserve to be remembered : " Thoughts
cannot be transferred : they must be appropriated."
In this matter of Bible study above all, the worth to
ourselves of the help we gain will be in proportion
to the labour we bestow on making it our own.
And this labour does not mean necessarily much
learning, or even a great deal of leisure.　It consists
rather in the pondering over and over again of a
deep thought or difficult passage until the light of a
new truth breaks through the obscurity.　Thus, and

thus only, do we make our own what the Bishop himself has called "the certainty of the assurance, which each day's work makes stronger, that Holy Scripture opens treasures new and old to men and to Churches, now as in former times, when the scribe becomes a disciple of the Kingdom of God." [1]

In these very words we have an instance of the way in which our reading must be carried on, to make it profitable. "A disciple of the Kingdom of God"—the phrase is so familiar that we are inclined, perhaps, to pass it over without any very close or resolute questioning as to what it actually means when applied to the study of the Scriptures. But if we "keep the saying, pondering it in our hearts," and question it again and yet again, determined not to let it go until we have gained a blessing from it, we find ourselves amazed at the greatness of that blessing when at last it is won. For once we have learnt what it is to study the Scriptures as a "disciple of the Kingdom of God," not in name, but in reality; searching their pages with a living desire ever to know more truly and to wield more strongly the sovereignty of our God; then we have made our own the secret which can transform our Bible study, and through it the whole of life.

[1] *Introduction to the Study of the Gospels*, Preface to 4th edition.

1. The Difficulties of Bible Study

We need no teacher to point these out to us, for indeed no earnest attempt at Bible study can be made without meeting them. But what we do need, and what Bishop Westcott can do for us with such striking clearness, is to know how to deal with them.

Also, in seeking help from any source, we need to know clearly what we are looking for, and what we may expect. One of the most frequent causes of disappointment in men or books is due to the fact that we ask from them a form of help which it is not their aim to give. It is useless, for instance, to look to Bishop Westcott for the help we so often long for, in *escaping* our difficulties; his purpose being always and only to show us how to *face* them. And if this is not what we are prepared to do—if what we are truly seeking is some "short cut" to Bible study, some clear and simple plan fully marked out for us to save us trouble—we shall turn to his books in vain.

For the Bishop never even attempted to supply such guidance; he did not believe in its value, and he mistrusted above all any endeavour to abolish the need for personal effort. Without such effort the study itself, to his mind, was robbed of half its value. On this point he was very definite.

"The Bible does not supersede labour"—he wrote, and insisted on the thought again and again in different forms—"but by its very form proclaims labour to be fruitful. . . . The Bible does not dispense with thought, but by its last message it lifts thought to sublimer regions. There is, no doubt, a restless desire in man for some help which may save him from the painful necessity of reflection, comparison, judgment. But the Bible offers no such help. It offers no wisdom to the careless, and no security to the indolent. It awakens, nerves, invigorates, but it makes no promise of ease. And by this it responds to the aspirations of our better selves. . . . Everything which makes life easier, makes it poorer, less noble, less human, less Godlike. What we need is not that the burden of manhood should be taken from us, but that we should be strengthened to support it joyously : not that our path should be made smooth and soft, but that it should be made firm to the careful foot : not that our eyes should be spared the vision of celestial glory, but that we should see it reflected in Him who, being Man and God, can temper it to our powers." [1]

In Bible study, as in all life, Bishop Westcott saw in the difficulties the very means, if rightly used, to rouse our hearts to keener efforts, and so to

[1] *Lessons from Work*, p. 148.

F

draw us into closer touch with God through our
Lord Jesus.   Thus, in another place, he wrote:

> "Christ draws near to us when humbly and
> honestly we ponder His Word. The study is
> difficult—far more difficult than we commonly
> suppose, and far more fruitful—but He illumi-
> nates the dark places, and through a better
> understanding of the letter guides us to a
> warmer sympathy with the spirit." [1]

Perhaps one might say that the first lesson that we
learn from Bishop Westcott in this matter of Bible
study is the absolute necessity for individual effort.
Without this, as he was never weary of pointing out,
no help from without can be of lasting value.   "The
truths which we hold are worth to us just what they
cost us and no more." [2]   Thus he summed up his
own teaching, in words which every professing Christian and would-be Bible student would do well to
lay to heart.

This is the thought chiefly emphasised in his first
great work on Bible study, the *Introduction to the
Study of the Gospels.*

> "If the essay has any value"—he wrote in the
> Notice to the fourth edition—"it lies chiefly, I
> believe, in the encouragement which it offers to
> students who desire to examine the records of
> our Faith with patient and devout trust in the
> Spirit of Truth."

And again, in another of the prefaces :—

---

[1] *Revelation of the Risen Lord*, p. 53.   [2] *Gospel of Life*, p. xxv.

"Nothing was further from my purpose than to supersede individual study. My whole object will have been gained if I have guided any fellow-students along paths in which labour is fruitful, to springs of thought which are ever fresh." [1]

Over and over again throughout the book he presses home upon his readers the same conviction, that personal study is the *only* key to unlock the treasures of the Scriptures, and that no teaching, however excellent, can take its place.

"The subtle organisation of Scripture, no less than that of nature, is only revealed to a watchful and attentive eye. A passing hint may arouse inquiry, but nothing less than a patient and candid study of the Bible can convey any notion of the intimate real relations which exist between its several parts." [2]

The lesson is surely one that we all need to master. In these days, especially, of short cuts to knowledge of every kind, and of labour-saving devices for the achievement of result without endeavour, it is well to set about our Bible study with the clear assurance that our gains will be in proportion to the reality of our efforts ; that according to the earnestness with which we give heart and soul and strength as well as time to the task, will be the certainty with which "we shall learn with a more loving endurance, and know with a more prevailing knowledge, that *whatsoever things were written afore-*

---

[1] *Introduction to the Study of the Gospels*, p. viii.   [2] *Ibid.* p. 34.

time were written for our learning, that through patience and comfort of the Scriptures we might have hope—a hope which enters within the veil, and rests in the calm of heaven." [1]

This necessity for personal effort, then, is the first lesson that Bishop Westcott would have us draw from the difficulties of Bible study ; and the next is the witness which these difficulties bear to the divine nature of the revelation contained in the Scripture records.

> " It was long since said : 'God was pleased to leave difficulties upon the surface of Scripture, that men might be forced to look below the surface.' " [2]

The revelation of things divine, eternal, and unseen, by human means, and to human minds, is necessarily a work fraught with difficulties. Through a glass, in a mirror, in a riddle—darkly, imperfectly, in part—such is, in the nature of things, the measure of our human vision of divine truths. To beings such as we are, therefore, the revelation of God's working must ever be hard to record, and not less hard to understand.

> " We must remember in the midst of the doubts and perplexities which so easily beset us, that at present *we know but in part* the facts and the bearings of Revelation. Dim views of a wider scope and a more perfect wisdom are ever opened before us. Faith looks forwards as well as inwards ; and even now we see enough whereon

[1] *Introduction to the Study of the Gospels*, p. 160.
[2] *The Bible in the Church*, p. x.

to rest securely the firm foundations of our hope, possessing our souls in peace, till *that which is in part shall be done away*—till the refulgent buildings of the New Jerusalem and its heavenly glories shall be fully disclosed, whereof at present we can but discern, amid the mists of earth, wondrous pillars and buttresses, or through some dim window the distant rays of that glorious Sun—even the Lamb of God—which shall at one time illumine the Holy City." [1]

Yet, though some difficulties Bishop Westcott would have us manfully to accept, as belonging to the nature of Bible study, there were some also which he considered that we make for ourselves, by using the Scriptures in a way, and for a purpose, for which they were never meant. We seek to discover from them the facts which we ourselves desire to know, instead of receiving from them the revelation which God has willed to give. This also comes as a new thought to many readers ; and here again it is well not to let it go until we have conquered its meaning. One step—and a great one—towards the transformation of our Bible study is gained when we have learned to go to the Scriptures " to receive, not to create," as the Bishop says elsewhere ; to try and gain from them not what we chance at the time to want, but what they were from the beginning meant to give. With the Gospels especially—the heart of all the Scriptures—it is wonderful to find how the difficulties of studying them disappear when we try to make it our purpose, for a while at any rate,

[1] *Introduction to the Study of the Gospels*, p. 409.

just simply to see and to accept the lessons they were written to teach *in the form in which we find them ;* treating them not as imperfect narratives of facts historically interesting, but as complete revelations of truths vitally important. " For Revelation *is not a vain thing for us ; it is our life.*" [1]

It is intensely hard to express this way of Bible study in any words that shall be intelligible to other minds. Perhaps the most practical suggestion that could be given to readers who have not already tried it, would be that they should take as a beginning, a single Gospel,—possibly St. Mark, as being in the simplest form,—and in reading it, that they should endeavour to put themselves always in the attitude of a learner towards his master ; trying, not to dictate for themselves the lessons they are to gain, but to realise and make their own those which the Evangelist desired to teach, in the order and in the form in which he has seen it best that they should be conveyed. Simply to hold in mind this purpose of learning from the writer in his own way, instead of determining for ourselves what and how he is to teach us, is in itself a marvellous help towards the understanding of the Scriptures. For it enables us to gain from them what they were meant to give, instead of putting them to uses for which they never were designed. It is a great point, therefore, to remember that in all true study of the Gospels, " the object of the student will be to follow out the course of each revelation of the truth, and not to frame annals of the Saviour's life." [2]

[1] *Introduction to the Study of the Gospels,* p. 45.
[2] *Ibid.* p. 351.

To teach this most important truth was one of Bishop Westcott's objects in his early and very brilliant work on Bible study, the *Introduction to the Study of the Gospels*. The first and last chapters set it before us with special clearness.

> "The New Testament does not contain a mere record of ordinary facts, or a collection of indifferent conclusions, but lays the historic groundwork of man's redemption, and builds up his practical faith." [1]

And again :

> "The Gospels are unchronological in order. We are at once cautioned against regarding them as *mere* history, and encouraged to look for some new law of arrangement in their contents, which, as I shall endeavour to prove, must result from a higher power than an unaided instinct or an enlightened consciousness." [2]

> "We have already noticed the error of those who contemplate the life of Christ, as recorded by the Evangelists, only outwardly, without regarding its spiritual significance. . . . The first step to a right understanding of the Gospels must be the abandonment of this point of sight ; we must regard them as designed to set forth the progress of a divine work embodied in the Son of Man ; we must read them to learn the details of our redemption, and not to add some new facts to the chronicles of the world." [3]

[1] *Introduction to the Study of the Gospels*, p. 24.
[2] *Ibid.* p. 23.   [3] *Ibid.* p. 400.

Such is the help that we can gain from Bishop Westcott's writings in the main difficulties which the study of the Bible offers. The value of that help is known to all who have tried it. Of the difficulties themselves the Bishop has said :

" Happy are they who have not felt them ; but happier, I think, are they who, feeling them, are led, by a discipline which is at first painful, to a wider, deeper, fuller view of Him *in whom are all the treasures of wisdom and knowledge, hidden* —hidden, in order that they may be revealed in due season, according to the needs of men." [1]

[1] *Christus Consummator*, Preface.

2. How to Regard the Bible as a Whole

It was Bishop Westcott's intense conviction—a conviction influencing all his teaching—that "no one indeed can make another feel what the Bible is: that assurance must come to each from the Spirit of God speaking to the single soul through the Word of God."[1] Yet reader after reader has learnt both to prize and study the Bible with new eagerness by learning from the Bishop's writings what he himself found there, and how he found it.

It is a not uncommon fancy that the intellectual study of the Scriptures weakens their spiritual force. Here was a profound scholar, whose life was spent in the most laborious examination of the text, and the minutest criticism, and he could say, when his labours were drawing to their close, that he had found in them "unfailing strength and light," in "every variety of circumstances."

"The Book itself forces us to go beyond the Book to a Person," he said in one of his addresses on the subject. "It constrains us to find the only rest of soul in Him whom it reveals. . . . No criticism can rob the Scriptures of this

[1] *Lessons from Work*, p. 151.

power. We do not think that we *have life in them*, but in Him of whom they witness."[1]

And again, elsewhere :

" We investigate what is written with unwearied diligence, not that we find rest there, but that we may follow the clue which it offers to guide to the Lord Himself (John v. 39). The words fail in their function if they do not lead us to the Word."[2]

" The words fail in their function if they do not lead us to the Word." The whole principle of Bishop Westcott's study of the Bible is given in that one sentence. To him the whole of the Bible was always and only the revelation, the veil, the glass, pieced together out of many parts, in divers fashions, half hiding, half disclosing God's eternal glory, on which our human weakness cannot gaze unveiled. "Through a glass, darkly"—the simile which he so often quoted—suggests the three ways in which the Bible can be studied, even as a glass can be viewed : by gazing *at* it, to catch our own reflection ; or *into* it, to examine its surface ; or *through* it, to discern what lies beyond. All three ways have their uses, and all are recognised by those who study the Bible with any earnestness. The characteristic of Bishop Westcott's teaching is the order in which he would have us place them. The great majority of ordinary readers seek in the Scriptures first and foremost the reflection of their own individual desires and needs.

---

[1] *Lessons from Work*, p. 137.
[2] *Some Thoughts from the Ordinal*, p. 22.

Students and critics, on the other hand, grow often all-engrossed in their minute examination of the surface of the records. Bishop Westcott, brilliant scholar and laborious student as he was, kept his gaze fixed always through and beyond the text at which he worked "with unwearied diligence," and with the one steadfast purpose of rendering more clear the vision of God's glory, seen through His written Word.

> "The glory of the Lord : the phrase is a key-word of Scripture ; the whole record of revelation is a record of the manifestation of God's glory. The Bible is one widening answer to the prayer of Moses, *Show me Thy glory*, which is the natural cry of every soul made for God. The answer does not indeed come as we look for it. We do not understand at first our own weakness. And so God has been pleased to make Himself known *in many parts and in many fashions*, by material symbol and through human Presence, as man could bear the knowledge." [1]

The passage is taken from the second of the three sermons in the Appendix to the *Revelation of the Father*. All three teach the same lesson—perhaps the best that the great scholar and saint could leave us. For it goes to the very heart of this matter of Bible study, as those know who have learnt to look away from themselves to God, and so to gain the fresh power which alone can *conquer* life's trials and perplexities. To keep these always

[1] *Revelation of the Father*, p. 164.

before us in our study of the Scriptures, is to look only at our own image in the glass, and in that there is little comfort. To make it our purpose to learn more of God's glory than of our needs, is to gaze through and beyond the earthly veil, and so to lose sight of self and selfish sorrows in the transcendent vision of the eternal Majesty and Love of God.

> " When we look inwards on self, we are apt to see nothing else : when we look outwards on the whole revelation which God has been pleased to make, self is transfigured into a part of a grander unity." [1]

We have a great truth here, and one that can do much for us. That one sentence expresses in its true form the principle borrowed from Christianity by many of the popular systems of "new religion," or "new thought." The dazzling promises wherewith these win their followers are nearly all based on this one idea of the conquest of weakness by the thought of strength. They work in new ways, and they offer new short cuts to success, which fall in with modern restlessness ; yet all the while they have not the true secret of lasting power which Bishop Westcott laid bare. For he bids us seek the strength which is to move the world, not from some vague, mysterious source within ourselves, according to a plan of our own devising, but from a personal, living, and unchanging God, and by the means that He Himself has chosen for His revelation. And among the foremost of these means the Bishop numbered the Scriptures which the Church

[1] *Religious Office of the Universities*, p. 26.

has treasured for us, and from which we can learn the attainment of the Will of God, which always answers to our true desires.

Truly the false systems soon would lose their power if those who "profess and call themselves Christians" would learn, as Bishop Westcott learnt and taught, to treat their Faith as a living and most practical force by which to remove mountains of difficulty, and conquer weakness, disease, and sin. Over and over again in his writings he shows how the Bible teaches this, as, for example, in an address to candidates for Ordination :

> " The Bible teaches us by showing how God dealt with men one by one, and how He dealt with nations. It lifts the veil, so to speak, from His hidden movements, and at the same time we hear the voice of innumerable witnesses telling of victories of Faith.
>
> " . . . The Bible is not merely the Charter of our Faith, written in a language obsolete and only half intelligible, but a message of the living God to struggling men. . . . We lose our highest privilege, we leave undone our proper work, unless we fix our eyes upon the glorious image, that we may ourselves reflect it, and show it to those who are committed to our care." [1]

The whole of the *Introduction to the Study of the Gospels* is directed to making clear the practical helpfulness of this way of looking upon the Bible throughout as God's revelation of Himself to man ;

[1] *Some Thoughts from the Ordinal*, p. 22.

and the same teaching is given in a shorter and simpler form in the Appendix already mentioned, to the *Revelation of the Father*. The first sermon of this series is specially well worth reading by all who find it hard to regard the Old Testament throughout in this manner. It is indeed to such readers that it is addressed.

" I wish to lead some who may be troubled by difficulties of detail in the Old Testament, to strive after a more comprehensive view of its character, to consider what St. John encourages us to call its spirit.

" There are difficulties in the Old Testament —difficulties which perhaps we cannot explain. We have no desire to extenuate or to hide them. It would be strange if we had: for it is through these, as we believe, that we shall in 'due time learn to know better God's way of dealing with us. But we are also bound to remember that the Old Testament offers to us something far higher, deeper, more majestic, more inspiriting than materials for literary problems. . . . It opens to us the prospect of one purpose variously reflected in writings spread over a thousand years : of one purpose moving onwards with a continuous growth among the barren despotisms of the east : of one purpose fulfilled in an unbroken national life which closed only when its goal was reached.[1]

" If then it is certain that the writings of the Old Testament offer to us many grave difficulties which we are at present unable to overcome, it

[1] *Revelation of the Father*, p. 149 *et seq.*

is no less certain that they offer a revelation of a purpose and a presence of God which bears in itself the stamp of truth. The difficulties lie in points of criticism : the revelation is given in the facts of a nation's life." [1]

The same thought also is dwelt on in the introduction to the Bishop's *Commentary on the Epistles of St. John.*

" . . . The study of Scripture is, I believe, for us the way by which God will enable us to understand His present revelation through history and nature. . . . The fulness of the Bible, apprehended in its historical development, answers to the fulness of life. If we can come to see in it the variety, the breadth, the patience of the past dealings of God with humanity, we shall gain that courageous faith from a view of the whole world which is commonly sought by confining our attention to a little fragment of it. . . .

" . . . As we look back and look forward in the light thus thrown over the world, we can work and wait." [2]

That we should learn to " work and wait," in patience, faith, and love, is surely one of the practical lessons that can be gained from any study. That it can be learned from the pages of the Bible has been *proved* again and again by readers of all kinds and degrees,—not necessarily rich either in scholarship or leisure,— who have accustomed themselves to

[1] *Revelation of the Father,* p. 158.
[2] *Epistles of St. John,* pp. vi.-viii.

looking upon the Scriptures as the veil " of many parts and many fashions " through which we can discern the vision of God's eternal glory. The vision is not always clear. It may be obscured here and there by flaws in the records, the earthly veil through which we view it. Or it may be clouded, far more often, by our own imperfect sight. Yet still, if we keep our gaze fixed steadfastly through clouds and dimness upon the light beyond, we shall discern enough, and more than enough, to kindle our love and longing for Him Who is our Life.

3. How to Study the Bible

Here we come to the heart of the whole matter. We have gained much—unspeakably much—when we have learnt to view the Scriptures in their true light, and confidently to face the perplexities which they present. Yet still the actual study of those Scriptures remains a difficult matter, and one in which we constantly feel the need of closer help and guidance. How hard it is, even with the most steadfast purpose, to make our Bible study always satisfactory, always "profitable for teaching, for reproof, for correction, for instruction which is in righteousness!" How well we all know the sense of disappointment that comes over us when we turn to the pages of the Bible, sometimes, as it seems, in vain ; and how earnestly we long for some one to mark out for us a connected line of thought, or help us to realise anew the power of the revelation.

All this is exactly what Bishop Westcott has done for us in his writings. He has marked out the general principles which should guide our reading, and he has shown us their application in detailed courses of study. While in his own example— perhaps the most precious legacy of all that he has left us—we have a striking proof of the power of those principles when carried into daily practice. He laboured for ten years at the revision of the New Testament, and at the end of it he wrote that he should count the time well spent if he had been enabled to help in any degree in bringing home to "English-speaking people in years to come" that one great thought of life "in Christ," to which the changes in the Revised Version give greater clearness.[1]

And for those who were disposed to count as wasted the labour spent on trifling changes, he had an answer ready.

> "I am at a loss to understand how any one can hold that it is a matter of indifference whether we say 'In Him were all things created,' or 'by Him.' Have we a right to limit a divine relation? Is it, again, a matter of indifference whether we say 'the free gift of God is eternal life in Christ Jesus,' or 'through Christ Jesus'? To me, I confess, it makes a fundamental difference in the whole conception of Christianity whether we regard life as something which Christ has won for us apart from Himself, or something which is absolutely bound up with Himself and only realised in vital fellowship with Him."[1]

So the Bishop spoke before the Convocation of York in answer to some criticisms on the changes made by the New Testament revisers in words of so-called unimportance.

[1] *Lessons from Work*, p. 169.

"I cannot venture," he insisted, "to choose either in Holy Scripture, or in any version of Holy Scripture, details which I regard as important, to the exclusion of others. This phrase or that may seem to me to be strange or uncouth, but I have a limited and imperfect vision. Let me then strive with absolute self-control and self-surrender to allow Apostles and Evangelists to speak in their own words to the last syllable, and the least inflection, in Hebrew idiom, and with Hebrew thought. Let them so speak, and let us humbly wait till in God's good time we are enabled to read the fulness of their meaning in our own tongue. I know no way in which we can understand the meaning of a message except by the patient observance of the exact words in which it is conveyed." [1]

In the same spirit he wrote in the *Introduction to the Study of the Gospels* :

"Before we pronounce any clause or word in the Bible insignificant or needless, let us be assured that it contains no *mystery* — that it teaches the humble student no new lesson in the knowledge of the world, or of man, or of God." [2]

And again :

"The connection of events, the arrangement of arguments, and the choice of symbols, may serve to exhibit in clearer and more varied outline the

[1] *Lessons from Work*, p. 169.
Introduction to the Study of the Gospels, p. 400.

whole structure of Christianity. For nothing
can be immaterial which is able to influence our
idea of the Saviour's life, or to alter the application of Christ's teaching." [1]

Thus Bishop Westcott practised himself, and
would have others practise, the closest possible attention to every detail of the text ; but always and only
" to learn the details of our redemption, and not to
add some new facts to the chronicles of the world." [2]

" The student may choose the field for his own
inquiries "—he says elsewhere—" with the certainty
of a rich harvest. Let him take any group of
lessons recorded in one of the Gospels—miracles,
parables, discourses—let him notice their salient
points and most minute traits : let him combine
them with similar recitals contained in other
Gospels : and his feeling will be a wonder, which
increases with time, at the fulness and sublety of
the connections by which each part of Holy
Scripture is bound to all others ; and this feeling
is the noblest homage to Inspiration.

" Any one who has arrived by patient and
individual labour at this sense of the absolute
significance of every part of the Bible, which is,
I believe, the sure reward of such a study of it
as I have described, will not rest satisfied with
its literal meaning only. The letter will never
lose its truth or its value, but it will be felt to be
the receptacle of a higher spirit." [3]

This first side of Bishop Westcott's teaching—

---

[1] *Introduction to the Study of the Gospels*, p. 24.
[2] *Ibid.* p. 400.　　　[3] *Characteristics of the Gospel Miracles.*

the need for close and careful study of the *text* of
the Scriptures—is perhaps most fully shown in the
Introduction to the Study of the Gospels, and in his book
on the *Revised Version of the New Testament*.   The
same thoughts are given more briefly in the three addresses on the subject included in *Lessons from Work*.

For the other lesson on which he insisted with
equal force—the need of importance of looking
always for the inner meaning hidden in the outward
details—we shall do better to turn to the practical
examples given in the Bishop's courses of study on
individual subjects.   Three books which form a
striking group of lessons are—*The Characteristics of
the Gospel Miracles*, *The Revelation of the Father*,
and *The Revelation of the Risen Lord*.

These are all written on the same plan and with
the same purpose.   In each the Bishop takes some
special series of our Lord's manifestations of Himself, and shows the progressive lessons to be learnt
from these by patient study of their separate details,
and of their sequence.   The three books form a
splendid course of Bible study in the order given
above ; and they have a further and an even greater
value in the fact that each is written to throw light
not merely on the subject dealt with, but through
its means on all study of the Scriptures.   This purpose is very clearly expressed in the preface to the
second edition of the *Revelation of the Risen Lord.*

" I have touched only upon one fragment of
the revelation which the Bible discloses ; but
the same method is applicable to every part.
If once we can see the variety, the breadth, the

long - suffering of the divine dealings with humanity, as portrayed in the Old and New Testaments in different ways, we shall gain that courageous faith for a view of the whole world which is commonly sought by confining attention to a little portion of it."

In the same way, in the *Characteristics of the Gospel Miracles*, Bishop Westcott sought to show the wealth of instruction, interest, and personal help to be gained from the study of the Gospels, or any portion of them, not as a record only, but as a revelation, not complete in itself, but a part of a larger whole, bound up with the rest, and inseparable from it.

" The miracles of the Gospel," he insisted, " are not isolated facts ; they are not vain repetitions. . . . The miracles are all faint reflections of the glory of the Incarnation. That is the miracle of miracles, to which all others point.[1] . . . By facts and not by words we are taught that there is a power in man, though not man's, able to do all things : that there is a future open to man in which he will reign through Christ over a redeemed world. The power is ours : the future may be ours. And surely, if the contest on which it hangs be hard, the prize is noble, and the hope is great. It may be that Christ will reveal Himself to us in losses, as he did to the Gadarenes : it may be that He will reveal Himself to us in blessings, as he did to St. Peter. However it be, He can transform the

[1] *Characteristics of the Gospel Miracles*, p. xi.

loss into a greater gain, and convert the blessing into the type of a higher work. The miracles are the sacraments of these heavenly realities ; and may God grant to us to carry the lessons of creation and providence, the lessons of a soul prevailing by union with its Saviour, to our common duties." [1]

Here once more is struck the prevailing note of Bishop Westcott's teaching ; the practical *using* of the deepest truths as a power in daily life. This is the thought insisted on throughout.

" As far as miracles are flashes of a heavenly life and power bursting through the thin veil of natural life, as far as they are revelations of the invisible, Epiphanies of the divine, they belong to all time. . . . The hindrance which checks our labours lies not in Christ but in us : not in the greatness of our distresses, but in the faintness of our aspirations. Those miracles speak to us of what men have done and gained in Christ, whose help outran their trust, of what men can do, for the promise is still unrecalled, even if it is unused. They speak to us of a power of faith which opens the eyes of the blind, and removes the stains of the impure. They speak to us of a power of prayer which gives utterance to the stammering tongue, and strength to the palsied limbs. They speak to us of a power of love which transcends all known laws and spoils the grave of its victim (P. 63 *et seq.*)

[1] *Ibid.* p. 93 *et seq.*

Thus it is that the Bishop throws light for us on the deepest teaching of the Gospel miracles. In his *Revelation of the Father* he has marked out another line of special study by showing

> " Some of the great lessons which are revealed to us in the titles of the Lord contained in the Gospel of St. John." (P. 3.)

In the study of those titles he believed that new and growing light would be found on the revelation of our Lord Jesus Christ, and through Him upon the whole of the Scriptures.

> " No one, unless I am mistaken, can consider the titles by which the Lord successively reveals Himself in the Gospel of St. John without acknowledging the naturalness of each revelation, and the growing light which they throw one after another in due order upon His work and upon His Person. Each title as it was used was intelligible. Each title when studied afterwards disclosed (and still discloses) fuller depths of meaning." (P. vi.)

The book needs to be studied throughout in order to appreciate, in their true sequence, the thoughts suggested on these titles of the Lord. Some idea, however, of their beauty, their depth, and their intensely personal helpfulness, may be gained from the next few passages on " The Way, the Truth, and the Life."

> " Men, I say, are perplexed. The infinite complexity, and hurry and intensity of modern

life, confuses our perceptions of its general tendency. The old paths appear to be lost in a wild maze. Eager voices call us to follow this track or that. If we pause for a moment, we are at once left behind by our fellow-travellers. There is no repose, no waiting for fuller knowledge. We are almost driven to ask if there be any way, any end at all before us ? And if there be, whether it is not hopeless for us to look for it ? At such times let us hearken to Christ's voice, *I am the Way*, and then purpose and order will come back to the world. We shall see that through all the ages there does run one way of self-sacrifice, and that way is Christ. . . .

" . . . We may not be able to tell whither we are going, but it is enough that Christ has bridged over the chasm between earth and heaven, and that as we advance along the way which He made, and which He is, we shall sooner or later be admitted to the vision of God and reflect the brightness of His glory. . . .

" . . . We have been placed upon the Way. We have been taught the Truth. We have been made partakers of the Life. The Way must be traversed : the Truth must be pursued : the Life must be realised. Then cometh the end. Our pilgrimage, long as it may be or short, if we have walked in Christ will leave us by the throne of God ; our partial knowledge, if we have looked upon all things in Christ, will be lost in open sight ; our little lives perfected, purified, harmonised in Him whom we have

trusted, will become in due order parts of the
one Divine Life, when God is all in all." (P. 111
et seq.)

The study of these eight titles of our Lord will
be found a helpful continuation to the study of His
miracles, and will lead on naturally to the careful
contemplation of the *power* of His Resurrection—
the crowning point alike of miracles and revelation
—which is the subject of the *Revelation of the Risen
Lord*.

The following practical suggestions on the study
of the Bible are all taken from the Bishop's address
on the subject in *Lessons from Work*.

"The study of Holy Scripture must be
systematic. . . . In making your plans for reading,
aim rather at securing perfect regularity than at
covering a large field. Fix your reading, I would
say, at half the amount which your fresh zeal
suggests. The punctual fulfilment of a small task
braces for greater effort. Gradual failure in the
fulfilment of an ambitious design leaves us per-
manently weakened and discouraged. Few com-
paratively know what is meant by the accumulated
result of the work of half an hour, or of the quiet
meditation on three or four verses every day
throughout a year.

". . . In your reading you must keep two objects
in view. Strive to gain familiarity with the broad
outlines of the arguments of several different books ;
and also seek to enter into the fulness of the
meaning of some special book. To this end read
one subject rapidly and another minutely. But

pause in each case to reckon up from time to time
what you have gained : what questions are left for
later answering : what occasions have been given
you for thanksgiving or prayer or confession.

". . . There is, we must all have felt, a singular
personality in the language of the Bible. . . . We
hear in the Scripture the living voices of living men
speaking to ourselves. It is not so equally with all
parts or at all times, because our own experience is
very limited and unequal, but still phrases of the
Bible startle us by their direct application to our
own wants, by their clear revelation of our own
thoughts : they cling, as it were, to us : they reach
where no friend's voice could reach : they stay
where even the counsel of love could find no
entrance. . . .

". . . And as the Bible speaks to us all severally,
and so claims our individual service, it speaks to us
also at each crisis of our spiritual growth. How
often it happens that a great sorrow or a great joy,
or the slow passage of years, makes sayings clear
which were dark before. And besides this, there is
a natural progress in our understanding of the
Scriptures. Some things we can see when we are
children : some things are opened to us in maturer
age : some things remain mysteries to the end.
But however slowly we go forward, or however
swiftly, voices of Scripture are always with us. It
is with the faithful student as with the manna-
gatherer in old times : He that gathers much has
nothing over, and he that gathers little has no lack."

Those who give time and patience to the
mastering of these thoughts—and, still more, to

carrying them into practice — find themselves
amazed at the transformation wrought in their
Bible-reading by the steadfast effort to study the
written Word of God, " not that we may find rest
there, but that we may follow the clue which it
offers to guide us to the Lord Himself." They
who have learnt so to study the Bible, have learnt
also that it is indeed " more than a book : it is the
voice of God answering to the voice of man."

" Blessed Lord, by whose Providence all Holy
Scriptures were written and preserved for our
instruction, give us grace to study them each day
with patience and love. Strengthen our souls
with the fulness of their divine teaching. Keep
us from all pride and irreverence. Guide us in
the deep things of Thy heavenly wisdom ; and,
of Thy great mercy, lead us by Thy Word into
everlasting life, through Jesus Christ our Saviour.
Amen." [1]

[1] *Common Prayers for Family Use*, p. 8.

V

CHURCH AND CREED

CHURCH AND CREED

I. THE CHRISTIAN CHURCH

"The Church of Christ calls all to its active service, and welcomes all with each power they bring. Every variety of intellect may find its scope. Every diversity of gift may find its consecration. . . . Think on what Christ has done in past ages through the noble army of His servants, and know by that what He will do for you."—*Words of Faith and Hope*.

"Our creed must be a spiritual growth, and not a dress."—*Lessons from Work*.

"It must in the end be disastrous to cherish a creed which finds no expression in our lives."—*Christian Life, Manifold and One*.

"The truths which we hold are worth to us just what they cost us, and no more."—*Gospel of Life*.

HERE we come to subjects not in themselves likely to attract so many readers as that of Bible study. For every professing Christian recognises at least the duty of studying the Scriptures, while many are content to accept their membership in the Church as a matter of course that needs no questioning, and frankly to confess their lack of interest in either creed or doctrine. If readers such as these should be tempted to pass over Bishop Westcott's writings on these subjects as useful only to scholars, they will run the risk of losing the very help they chiefly need.

For this is what he teaches us above all, and through all : to recognise—even if it be to some of us still only as a far-off vision—what the Christian Church and the Christian Creed are in themselves ; what they might be in our lives.

A devoted student of Bishop Westcott's writings dates not only the introduction to these, but also a new era of thought and effort, from the reading "by chance," as we say carelessly, of the sermon on the "Kingdom of God" in *Social Aspects of Christianity*. In the thought of the Church as pictured there with the reality of intense conviction—in all its imperial splendour as an actual, living, and most glorious *Kingdom*—was opened up a whole new world of thought and hope and possibilities hitherto undreamed of in a faith professed as a matter of course.

There is of course no certainty that the same impression will be produced on other minds ; yet it can be scarcely possible to read without some thrill of enthusiasm such words as these :—

"As a King Christ received His earliest homage in the manger at Bethlehem. As a King He died 'reigning from the Cross.' The message which His herald was commissioned to proclaim, the message with which He Himself opened His Ministry, was the advent of the Kingdom. After His Resurrection He spoke with His disciples the *things pertaining the Kingdom of God*. And they in turn carried the glad tidings wherever they went beyond the borders of Judæa. It was of a Kingdom St. Philip spoke at Samaria:

of a Kingdom St. Paul spoke at Antioch, Thessalonica, Ephesus. And the last historic glimpse which we have of the apostolic working, shows us the same 'prisoner of the Lord' preaching the Kingdom of God in his captivity at Rome. In every part of the New Testament, in every region of early Christian labour, the teaching is the same. The object of Redemption is set before us not simply as the deliverance of individual souls, but as the establishment of a Divine Society : the saving not only of man but of the world : the hallowing of life, and not, characteristically, the preparation for leaving it." [1]

This last is a sentence to be pondered again and again, containing as it does the very heart of the Bishop's teaching. The glory which the Christian Faith can shed upon our lives *now* : the joy of the Church as a means of joining us together, here on earth, as " one man in Christ Jesus " : above all, His power and sovereignty over our lives as a practical experience of every day,—these were the thoughts by which Bishop Westcott lived his own life, and which he strove to share with all whom he taught.

" Thus the Gospel of Christ was in its announcement and in its preparation, as it is in its essence, the *Gospel of a Kingdom.* To *seek the Kingdom of God and His righteousness* is enjoined upon the believer as his first duty, and we ourselves, at least in word, acknowledge the obligation. Morning and evening we all pray in Christ's own words that ' Our Father's King-

---

[1] *Social Aspects of Christianity*, p. 85.

dom may come, on earth as in heaven ' : that it
may *come*, not that we may be carried away to
it far off, out of this stormy tumult of common
cares to some tranquil haven of rest : that it
may come to us on earth as in heaven."

To many of those who have never before considered the subject with special seriousness, this last
thought comes with all the force of a striking and
new idea.   It is abundantly well worth pondering
until its meaning is fully grasped.   For from that
vision of a Kingdom—a sovereignty, a new and prevailing power attainable here and now—is shed a
glory that can transform the whole of life.

And the vision, Bishop Westcott is careful to
insist, is no mere poet's dream.

> "The Kingdom of God is at once spiritual
> and historical : eternal and temporal : outward
> and inward, visible and invisible." [1]

It is all this, because Christ came " to deal with
the whole of life ; with thought, action, feeling—
with life in its largest and noblest forms, with life
in every phase of its progressive activity.   He came
to bring a message to the strong and the wealthy
and the gay, as well as to the weary and the heavy-
laden.   He came to found a Kingdom into which
the Kings of the earth should bring their glory."

> "*And for us,*" here is the assurance essential
> above all others to be grasped, "*that Kingdom
> of Heaven, the Kingdom of God, the Kingdom of
> the Son of Man, is a present reality.*" [2]

Social Aspects of Christianity, p. 88.   [2] *Ibid.* p. 89.

We have first of all to realise it as a living, practical fact of the closest possible concern to every one among us ; to ask ourselves what the Kingdom of God means to us in our daily lives ; and then comes the further question—what is our part in it ?

Here also the Bishop has an answer for us.

> " We are not called "—he says—" to found, but to *receive a Kingdom,* a Kingdom *that cannot be shaken.* Our part is only to offer ourselves to the divine influence by which we are surrounded ; to listen to the still voice which speaks to our souls with whisperings which if they cannot be uttered yet cannot be understood : to use the powers of a new age."

And the intense appeal which follows speaks to every heart :

> " Oh, my friends, life is vaster, immeasurably vaster, than we think—richer in resources, more fertile in strength, more blessed in opportunity. The glory of the Lord is still about the pilgrim's path : the Saviour, in His Spirit, is still with us, though *our eyes are holden that we should not know Him.* . . .
>
> " . . . We are come into the city of the living Lord, the heavenly Jerusalem ; but our sight is dim, and our faith is feeble. Lord, we pray Thee, open our eyes that we may see." [1]

The two sermons which follow deal with two characteristic efforts of the past to embody this thought of the Church of Christ as a *Kingdom* in an

[1] *Social Aspects of Christianity,* p. 98.

open and outward form, suited to the different times in which they were made. In both cases the Bishop traces the reasons alike of their partial success and partial failure, forming out of these the inspiring vision of a more perfect effort still to be made.

The sermon on this last was preached on St. Stephen's Day, and concludes with words of a hope kindled afresh in the light of the Incarnation.

> " Live at any rate, however hard it is, as Christians, as citizens of that Kingdom of which the notes are *righteousness, peace, joy*. Confess gladly that the Gospel has not only strong consolation for those whose work is well-nigh over, but, even more essentially, inspiration for those whose work is yet to be done. Let nothing rob you of the conviction that the voice of God can be heard, and is heard, ' *To-day* ' : that the vision of God can be gained, and is gained, ' To-day.' Keep the eyes of your heart fixed, not for the present on the Christ pierced and bleeding on the tree, but on the Risen Christ, reigning on the Father's throne. Look upward, eager to live, ready to die for Him ; and you too, like St. Stephen, will see *the heavens opened* —see the communion of the visible and the invisible restored ; you will see *the glory of God* —see a fresh manifestation of His purifying, quickening love. . . ." [1]

The deeper students of Bishop Westcott's works are sometimes unwilling to let his teaching be re-

---

[1] *Social Aspects of Christianity*, p. 152.

presented by passages taken from what they term his "popular" works; protesting that these do not adequately represent so profound a scholar. They do not of course display the wide range of his learning, yet the thoughts which filled his soul were always the same, whether expressed in commentary or sermon; and the purpose of this book is to show the practical value of those thoughts to ordinary readers, rather than the depth of scholarship which is already known to all who have the training to appreciate it. Students, and those who have access to the Bishop's larger works, can follow out in these the more detailed development of the self-same teaching.

The *Commentary on the Epistles of St. John*, for instance, contains, in addition to the notes on the text, a masterly essay at the end on "The Two Empires: the Church and the World," in which this thought of the Church of Christ as a Kingdom is worked out more fully, in contrast and comparison with the Kingdom of the World, as embodied in the Roman Empire. There is intense interest in the picture drawn of the growth and development, side by side, of the two great and rival sovereignties—— the one claiming an outward, the other an inward dominion over men.

The same essay is also valuable as laying stress as well on the other side of the Bishop's teaching, which should never be ignored. To picture him as looking upon the Church solely in its outward aspect as a Kingdom is to lose half the meaning of his message. For to him the Church was also and always not less closely present in its personal power.

as the Body of Christ, in which all Christians were made one with Him, and through Him with one another. It is because the thought of the *Kingdom* of Christ — His outward and visible sovereignty among men — is so often overlooked that Bishop Westcott insisted upon it with such especial force. To quote from this essay on the " Two Empires ":

" The distinctness with which we have learnt to realise our personal responsibility and personal relationship to God in this last age of the Church has brought with it some drawbacks, and this is one of them, that the sense of a visible Kingdom of God on earth, established in righteousness and embracing all the fulness of humanity, has been deadened.

" Still the two aspects of the Faith—the individual and the social—are not only reconcilable : they are complementary. Each is necessary to the completeness of the other. The individual view tends to selfishness and isolation, when the larger scope of redemption is neglected ; the social view tends to enthusiastic dreams, when the need of the transfiguration of every power of man is forgotten. . . .

" . . . The faith in ' Christ a King '—the terms are practically synonymous — is still retained, and so it must always be. The Christian Creed cannot stop short of a social realisation. It deals with men not as isolated units but as members of a commonwealth."

The passages tracing the growth of the " Two Empires " side by side are of intense interest. They

should be read in full to be appreciated ; the following quotation will only serve to show the general line of thought :

> " It is, then, quite true to say that two empires, two social organisations, designed to embrace the whole world, started together in the first century. The one appeared in the completeness of its form : the other only in the first embodiment of the vital principle which included all after-growth. But the two empires had nothing in common except their point of departure, and their claim to universality. In principle, in mode of action, in sanctions, in scope, in history, they offer an absolute contrast. The Roman Empire was essentially based on positive law ; it was maintained by force ; it appealed to outward well-doing ; it aimed at producing external co-operation or conformity. The Christian Empire was no less essentially based on faith : it was propagated and upheld by conviction : it lifted the thoughts and working of men to that which was spiritual and eternal : it strove towards the manifold exhibition of one common life. The history of the Roman Empire is from the first the history of a decline and fall, checked by many noble efforts and many wise counsels, but still inevitable. The history of the Christian Empire is from the first the history of a victorious progress, stayed and saddened by frequent faithlessness and self-seeking, but still certain and assured though never completed." (P. 253.)

This thought of the Church of Christ as a *King-dom* is not an easy one to grasp in all its fulness. Partly because of the exclusively *local* sense in which we habitually use the word to denote a territory rather than a power. It sometimes is a help towards reaching the deeper meaning of the term, to look through the passages where it occurs in the New Testament, substituting some synonymous expression wherever this can be done. The " dominion," or " sovereignty," or " kingship " of Christ are in many cases what is meant by His " Kingdom," and to realise this often adds fresh force to a familiar phrase. These writings of Bishop Westcott's, too, as has been said already, have been the source of new light to many of their readers. But no external suggestions or teaching can take the place of the earnest and continued pondering of the thought, not only in the mind, but in the heart as well. Of all the Bishop's teaching, perhaps nothing is worth more to us than the reminder, already quoted, that " the truths which we hold are worth to us just that which they cost us, and no more."

2. The Christian Creed

The Christian Church was to Bishop Westcott before all things a *Kingdom*; the Christian Creed was to him before all things the *watchword* of that Kingdom—the declaration of loyalty to its King, prized as well as professed by every faithful subject. This was what he insisted on most strongly in all his teaching upon the Creed—its personal *value* to each individual Christian.

Here, as in every subject with which he dealt, the Bishop's learning goes often far beyond the depth of many of his readers; but the lessons which it was his constant aim to learn and teach speak to the needs of every heart. For they make clear just that which many of us question and seek in vain—the spiritual, practical, and intensely *personal* value of the Christian Creed, as an inspiration and support in the life and work and problems of every day.

" We on our part "—he said in his first address to his Diocese—" must match our thought and our efforts with our Creed. Yes, with our Creed. We shall not do our work by explaining away or minimising its central mystery, but by showing that this mystery includes the realisation of the loftiest desires of man, while it interprets and satisfies the age-long prophecies of nature and life." [1]

And again, in another address :

"We lose more than we know because we do not habitually meditate on the grandeur of our Creed. . . . That the divine revelation may become the master force of our whole being, we must dwell upon it. We must regard that most solemn presence of the Father in Christ with lingering, loving gaze, till each detail becomes significant to us according to the plane which we occupy in the order of Providence. We must see it with our own eyes and not another's. . . ." [2]

To make clear this power of the Christian's Creed over his daily life was the Bishop's purpose in his *Historic Faith*, as we learn from himself in the preface.

". . . It was my object to show the direct bearing of the different articles of our Historic Faith upon our view of the world and of life. . . . The facts of the Divine Life reach with a present force to all life : they reach to our life. . . . It has been my desire to indicate what seem to me to be our obligations in asserting and extending the claims of the Faith, as calling to its service not one class of virtues or one type of character or one type of work, but all virtues, all characters,

[1] *Incarnation and Common Life*, p. 12.
[2] *Christus Consummator*, p. 86.

and all works, in the fulness of their distinctive energies, and according to the forms of their most effective operation. . . . If any thought which is suggested here is allowed to make more clear the living force with which our Faith deals with the doubts, the difficulties, the speculations the hopes of to-day ; to inspire one fellow-worker with a new confidence in maintaining a conflict where each victory must disclose fresh fields to conquer . . .—that will be a full reward for anxious reflection." [1]

How amply that reward has been reaped is shown by the large circle of readers by whom the book has been welcomed.[2] In form of expression it is one of the simplest of the Bishop's writings, the series of Lectures which it contains being short and easy to follow. In them he sets before us, first, the value of our Christian Creed as a whole, and afterwards the personal force and meaning of each article in succession.

The first Lecture, on " Faith," gives the key-note to the whole, in setting before us the possibility, and the urgent need, of seeking God in and through every means of help which He bestows.

" Before we can speak of a Creed, of the object of Faith, we must speak of Faith itself, which is the life of Creeds. The Creed is the word, but Faith is the power which appropriates it.

" What then is Faith ? If I were to say that it is the absolute condition of all life, of all action, of all thought which goes beyond the

<hr>

[1] Pp. v. vi.   [2] The 6d. edition of 1904 is the 7th edition issued.

limitations of our own minds, I should use no
exaggeration. . . .

" . . . Belief deals with that which has been or
with that which now is.   Faith claims as its
own that which is not yet brought within the
range of sense.   It is clear then that we cannot
get quit of our dependence upon Faith by doing
away with Religion.   We live by Faith however we live.   Perhaps, it is a sad possibility,
we can die without it." [1]

And, again, the same thought, with fresh
emphasis :

" Faith is in every age, under all circumstances,
that by which man lays hold on the realities
which underlie the changeful appearances of
things, and gives substance to hope—that by
which he enters into actual communion with
the powers of the unseen world and brings their
manifestation to a sovereign test.   It is the
harmony of reason, and feeling, and purpose.   It
is, to say all briefly, thought illuminated by
emotion and concentrated by will." [2]

What Faith *is*—that is what we need first to
realise, and then we have to go on to see with equal
clearness what it *is not*.   Here again Bishop Westcott
speaks with no uncertain sound :

" Credulity is not Faith.   That indolent abdica-
tion of the responsibility of judgment in favour
of every pretender, that superficial assent lightly
given and lightly withdrawn, is utterly at vari-

[1] Lecture I.   [2] *Ibid.*

ance with the intense, clear vision and with the resolute grasp of Faith.

"Superstition is not Faith. To choose for ourselves idols, whatever they may be, to invest with attributes of the unseen world fragments of this world, to brood over shadows, is to deny Faith, which is at every moment active, progressive, busy with the infinite.

"Conviction is not Faith. We may yield to what we admit to be an inevitable intellectual conclusion. Our opposition may be silenced or vanquished. But the state of mind which is thus produced is very often simply a state of exhaustion and not of quickening. Till the heart welcomes the Truth, it remains outside us." [1]

And then, having pondered what Faith is, and what it is not, comes the still more vital question, *What is Faith to us*—"this sovereign power which can see, use, dwell in the heaven which lies about us still?"

"Our answer to that question is the revelation of our life. It cannot be lightly made, and it cannot be wisely refused. It will show us what we aim at doing, and what we can do. It will find expression not in word but in deed.

"What is Faith to us? Perhaps as we come to feel more distinctly what it is capable of being, we shall answer best, mindful of our selfishness, of our triviality, of our forgetfulness of God, by praying that whatever it is it may hereafter be much more." [2]

[1] Lecture I.   [2] *Ibid.*

So from the thought of Faith as the master-power of life, we find ourselves led on naturally to consider the Creeds in which it finds expression. These form the subject of the second Lecture, which opens as follows :—

> " We have seen that every life is guided by Faith of some kind so far as it is of necessity directed to the future and unseen. And Faith implies a Creed. The Creed may be earthly, mean, debasing ; but no man can be without a Creed by which he shapes his conduct. . . .
>
> " . . . Thus the man of business and the man of pleasure has a Creed which is the strength of his life. The Christian also has his proper Creed. His Faith has an object wider, deeper, vaster, more enduring than the objects of form and sense, of which all that *is* is but a shadow and a sign. He believes not in a principle or a thought but in a Person ; not in himself or in mankind, but in the Lord Jesus Christ. . . ." [1]

And this belief, for the Christian, needs to be definitely expressed.

> " A form of words embodies, so to speak, the unseen object of our Faith. The citizen of the world is not called upon to put his Creed into set language. In many cases he would shrink from doing so ; and under any circumstances that which he prizes — wealth, rule, glory — is open to all eyes. There is no need to recall such things to the thoughts of those who have their faith in them. But with spiritual objects

[1] Lecture II

it is otherwise. Here we require to remind ourselves and to remind one another of the Invisible in which we trust : to bring this which we cannot handle or measure within the range of constant experience : to claim for it a place among the recognised powers of life." [1]

So we are shown the *necessity* for a Creed, and then are called upon to realise—still more tremendous thought—its power.

"It is this knowledge to which 'we have been delivered,' that it may mould and keep us— body, soul, and spirit—until the day of the Lord.

"*To which we have been delivered.* It is a most startling phrase ; yet this is literally what St. Paul says when he speaks of the Christian Creed. He does not write : *ye obeyed from the heart that form of doctrine which was delivered you*—that is but a small part of the truth—but *that form of doctrine whereunto ye were delivered.* The phrase is as startling as it is openly true. Our Creed, whatever it really is, is our sovereign master, or rather our inspiring power. It calls out our energies. It directs their application. It exacts our service. We can have no escape from its dominion : no rest from its influence. 'We are delivered to it' : perhaps as the un-conscious victims of a degrading thraldom, perhaps as the eager servants of that which we have gladly recognised to be a Divine Will." [2]

To those who grasp it for the first time, it is

[1] Lecture II.   [2] *Ibid.*

amazing to find how this thought of the *power* of
our Creed, as an active and practical force in our
daily life, thrills with new interest the study of its
different parts. To quote again the Bishop's words :—

> " Feeling then what a Creed is, what our Creed
> is, we approach the study of its contents with
> surer confidence, in order that we may learn
> better that it is able to guard, to support, to
> animate us : that it has strength to fashion our
> lives in health and sickness, in joy and sorrow,
> in thought and action, after a godlike type :
> strength to correct us with the authority of an
> inviolable law : strength to fill us with the
> enthusiasm of a living Faith." [1]

These two first Lectures deal solely with the
preliminary study of Faith and Creeds ; the remain-
ing nine follow out the teaching of the different
Articles of the Apostles' Creed in detail, one by one.
From these no passages are quoted, as they must be
studied thoroughly in order to appreciate to the full
the beauty, and the depth, and personal application
of the thoughts which they suggest. Only the concluding summary may be given, gathering up as it
does into a few sentences the outcome of the teaching
of the book.[2]

> " Thus it is that the cycle of our Creed is com-
> pleted. ' From God, unto God ' is the sum of
> the history which it discloses, wrought out once

[1] Lecture II.

[2] The Notes at the end are very full, and of great value to those
who are able to carry on the study further, and to enter into deeper
questions of scholarship.

for all in the human Life of the Son of God, and through the Spirit being still wrought out by His power in the world. The more we ponder over the facts which we confess in the fullest light of all the phenomena which it has been given to us to observe, the more surely shall we find that these facts of the Christian Creed cover the area of human life, of action, and of thought.

" They confirm to us a view of the future, which reconciles the contrasts of the present : they reveal to us a view of the present, which, while it intensifies the motives for personal exertion, adds a calming faith in the sovereignty of the Divine Will. They show us that there is an eternal significance in our daily struggles, failures, attainments, and that there is a goal for all being : they show us that we are fashioning day by day not ourselves only, but the society to which we belong. They take nothing from the value of the individual soul, and yet they disclose a life immeasurably vaster in which ' the many ' shall share.

" To the last we see little, and we see dimly. When the vision seems to grow clearer we are forced by our earthly infirmity to bow the head and veil the face before the exceeding glory. But in the Person of the Lord Jesus Christ we can see the Father. That is enough.

" OF HIM AND THROUGH HIM AND UNTO HIM ARE ALL THINGS. TO HIM BE GLORY FOR EVER. AMEN."

VI

WORSHIP

WORSHIP

I. CHURCH SERVICES

" Pray that in every act of worship, and in every deed of service, you may look with the eyes of your heart enlightened to a living, loving Lord, who is Himself the end of every form of earth which He hallows, and of every ministry of earth which He inspires."—*Christian Aspects.*

" Only let us be sure that religion is the consecration of our whole nature, and not the special attribute of any one part of it : only let us come to God such as we are, bowed down, it may be, with the burden of toil and care, without the opportunity, as it seems, of preparing an offering for His acceptance : and He will welcome and purify and hallow all that we lay before Him."—*Christian Life, Manifold and One.*

" The praise of God is the soul and inspiration of worship."— *Christian Aspects.*

" We know not what we ask, but we can ask that the will of God, which is our truest will, may be welcomed and fulfilled by and in us." —*Life of Bishop Westcott.*

To realise the eternal, to make the Presence of God a living, personal *fact* in our experience, to bring the power of the unseen to bear, as a practical force, upon the details of our daily lives — this was, in Bishop Westcott's view, the purpose of all worship. His teaching upon this subject runs through all his writings, as the thought of it ran through all his work. For to him it meant not merely the performance of certain duties, but the hallowing of every effort.

" Religion is not an accessory, as it were, to life— it is the soul of life." [1]

And again :

" The vision of God is indeed the transfiguration of the world : communion with God is the inspiration of life." [2]

To him one of the most distinctive notes of worship was that it " claims as the one prevailing force for the discharge of common duties, *in the name of the Lord Jesus*. It claims as the one dominant end of the most ordinary acts, *to the glory of God*. . . . We cannot be Christians in fragments," he insisted again and again. " Christianity finds expression in a Christian life, and not simply in Christian acts." [3]

Not that Bishop Westcott for a moment ignored the value of special acts and forms of worship. On the contrary, he was continually pointing out the need of these, to gather up into a definite and carefully directed force aspirations that otherwise might grow lifeless and vague. Only, to accomplish this, he taught that three truths above all others had to be grasped :—

1. That our Church Services should be looked upon as a source of power, *and used as such*.
2. That the responsibility for making them such rests with the people as much as with the priests.
3. That in order to fulfil this responsibility, the

---

[1] *Words of Faith and Hope*, p. 162.
[2] *Incarnation and Common Life*, p. 321.   [3] *Ibid*. p. 397.

Services need to be carefully *studied* by all who take part in them.

1. The *power* of the Church's Services is made clear in the words which follow :

" If in humble and faithful expectation we lay ourselves open to the divine influence, as we do to the air and the sunshine, not attempting to define too curiously how it quickens us : if we who teach, sink ourselves utterly in the message with which we are charged, and the ministry which we have to fulfil : if you who hear look beyond the voice and the instrument to Him whose love is brought so near you : if all come to this place prepared to receive and not to create : to offer themselves and to find life and access of life,—then we shall understand by fellowship with the Author of all strength what it is to confess and to know that *our sufficiency is of God*." [1]

2. The *responsibility of the Congregation* was a thought which the Bishop touched on many times ; never, perhaps, with more force than in one of his Ordination addresses, from which the next passage is taken.[2]

" Priest and people act and react one upon the other. They suffer together, they advance together. If it is true, as we all must admit, that the priest must use for his people every grace of the Spirit with which he is

---

[1] *Christian Life, Manifold and One*, p. 47.
[2] *Gifts for Ministry* (concluding address).

endowed, it is no less true that the people on
their part must use for their priest that seven-
fold gift which they too received by the
Apostolic laying on of hands. To them also is
entrusted a stewardship of sacred treasures by
which those that have rule over them must be
supported.

"This truth, this vital truth, has, I think, been
commonly overlooked ; and there has followed,
naturally, on the one side an assumption of
lordship, and on the other side a suppression
of spiritual force."

Then comes the special appeal, made with all
the solemnity of the approaching Ordination.

"In a little while you, my brethren of the
laity, will hear from their own lips how those
who offer themselves for the Ministry regard
their life's work and their calling ; you will hear
their aim, their resolution, their spring of confidence. And when you are afterwards required
to pray for the fulfilment of their desires, I do
not doubt that you will offer from your hearts
these supplications to God for them which you
feel are most rightly asked. But do not rest
satisfied with the passing act. Let your present
experience be the revelation of a continual
duty. Welcome the command of the earliest
manual of Christian practice, and let your
prayer rise night and day for him that speaketh
to you the Word of Life."

In the last address of the Appendix to *Christian*

Aspects, the same appeal is urged, and emphasised with a searching question.

"The work of the laity in the ministry of the Word, though the saying may sound like a paradox, is not less important than in prayer and praise. The teacher depends upon the people even as the people depend upon the teacher. . . . There must be co-operation between speaker and hearer if the Word is to be fruitful. Real gain here, as everywhere, is proportional to the effort made to secure it. . . . Dare we say that those in the Congregation who intercede for the preacher are as many as those who criticise him? Is it not possible that the Congregation may be in fault if the sermon fails in power?" (P. 428.)

And yet again—pressing the sense of personal responsibility ever more and more closely home upon each individual soul:

"The spiritual power of public worship depends, I repeat, on the temper of the Congregation. We can all feel when the Congregation is praying and not languidly following words of prayer: if we are cold the fire is kindled within us by their still fervour. Whatever may be our failures and faithlessnesses, no one of us can doubt what Common Prayer may become to us, and what it may do for us, when we remember the Lord's words: *If two of you shall agree on earth as touching anything that they shall ask, it shall be done for them of my Father which is in heaven.*" (P. 426.)

3. This same address sets before us also the value of a careful *study* of our Church Services, as a means of gaining a fuller, deeper sense of their power.

"Services which have a history of more than fifteen centuries, and reflect various phases of thought, cannot but require careful study if we are to enter into the fulness of their meaning. If confession, and thanksgiving, and praise, and hearing the Word, and prayer—to take the parts of public worship as they are enumerated in the General Exhortation—are severally difficult, it is evident what need there is of sustained reflection if we are to master the lessons which lie in the peculiar combinations in which they are provided for our use in our Prayer Book. Minister and Congregation alike must spare no pains to possess themselves of the hidden treasures which are offered for their quest.

"But may I not say with truth that the want of serious preparation for public worship robs our Services of their proper energy and warmth—widely different from personal emotion—which spring from the sense of a corporate life? Many recognise that public worship is a duty, but few, it is to be feared, look to it as their highest privilege; few realise the awful majesty of the solemn gathering; few feel when they take their place in the Congregation that (in the words of a great teacher) 'no other assembly in the world is so august.' Those who come together look rather to obtaining personal benefits than to offering worship to God, to receiving, rather than to giving ; and, even so, they make for the most part no adequate effort to gain the moral attitude which befits the expectation of a blessing.

"Such a temper necessarily affects the whole character of the Service, and is utterly alien from the spirit of our Offices. In these two thoughts are dominant : the thought of the majesty of God, and the thought of the manifold wants of our fellow-men with whom we are united : the thoughts, that is, of praise and of sympathy. The thought of self falls entirely into the background.

"It could hardly fail to be profitable to trace in detail throughout the Services these ruling ideas. The theme of praise is given out in the first versicle and response, 'O Lord, open Thou our lips : and our mouth shall show forth Thy praise,' followed by the Gloria. It is developed in the Venite : and the recurring Gloria after Psalm and Canticle reminds us that all the changes of life, all the varieties of experience, all the fluctuations of feeling, have one dominant purpose, that in them we may find God and recognise His will with glad submission." (P. 425.)

The purpose of all such study, as the Bishop makes abundantly clear, being " to lead to a fuller perception of the meaning and the power of our Common Prayer ; and through that to a deeper sense of the manifold presence of God about us." (P. 428.)

The whole of this address (a very short one)
should be read carefully, and the three addresses on
" The Congregation," " Common Prayer," and " The
Church," in *Words of Faith and Hope*, are also well
worth referring to on the subject.   So also is the
very beautiful third chapter in *The Revelation of the
Father*, on " The Bread of Life," touching as this
does upon the highest act of Christian worship.
Here also, from contemplating the deepest meaning
of the Eucharist, Bishop Westcott comes back
to the practical question of its influence upon the
worshipper's daily life.

> " And then from the Holy Communion we can
> go forth to our common life, which is shown to
> us as all hallowed in that Sacrament, most
> universal and at the same time most personal,
> and be assured that Christ will be ever with us :
> He in us, that we may never despair when we
> are beset by difficulties ; we in Him, that when
> we have attained something we may reach
> forward to greater victories." [1]

[1] *Revelation of the Father*, p. 42.

2. Sunday Observance

Thus it is that Bishop Westcott helps us to discern the spiritual realities of our acts of worship; nor does his teaching fail us when we go on to the difficult and disputed question of Sunday observance. His thoughts about Sunday are perhaps most clearly expressed in a sermon on "The National Day of Rest," included in *Christian Aspects of Life*, and they meet the anxious questionings of many hearts.

For it was straight to the heart that he spoke, seeing as he did in Sunday the answer to the heart's deepest needs. To him it was before all things "the new Sabbath"—the *day of the rest of the heart*, as an Assyrian tablet interprets the ancient word.

> "The Sabbath is the day of rest of the heart—this is the thought which I ask you to make your own." (P. 121.)

So Bishop Westcott strove to draw the minds of his hearers at once above and beyond the mere question of outward observances; and then went on characteristically to make clear the reason of his appeal.

> ". . . For the Sabbath is not simply in a negative sense a time in which we must refrain

from work for our own gain. It is that, but it
is more. . . .

"The Christian Sabbath is a season for entering, as we may be enabled, into the mind of
God ; for fulfilling, as He gives us power, His
work ; for *doing good* even as Christ did in the
place of religious assembly, in the home, in the
hospital, by the wayside, to those who are
suffering, and in whom the Divine Will has
not yet had its accomplishment. Our Rest-
day is the opportunity not only for a religious
exercise, but for the rendering of a solid portion
of our life to God. It is emphatically *the Lord's
Day*, the Rest-day of the Resurrection, in which
it is given us to realise the power of the new
life." (P. 125.)

That was the thought above all others on which
the Bishop loved to dwell, and it is a thought which
many of us sorely need to grasp — the Faith of
Christ as a living and transforming power, to be
realised and made our own in hours of quiet
thought, and to be used in the stress of daily
life.

"If we reflect on our nature and our position,
we shall at once feel our want of this 'rest of
the heart.' Mere repose, amusement, physical
pleasure, brings no real restoration to the toiler
wearied by a week of heavy labour. They all
belong to the same order as our daily work.
They cannot convey the invigorating force of
new influences — they open no fresh springs in the
parched soul. I would not underrate the effects

of literature, of art, of culture, of science; but they demand a heavy price for their ennobling lessons. Many of us cannot pay it; and God shows to us a loftier and a better way. He offers Himself to us, the source of all goodness, and truth, and beauty, to be reached by the affections. That way we all know, we all have followed." (P. 126.)

Rest of the heart brought within reach of all of us by Sunday — that is the first lesson; and the next is the intense need which we all have of such rest.

". . . Our Rest-day then, I say, is given to us to bring calm into the hurry of life. We are, most of us, restlessly busy — busy it may be with serious occupations, or busy with the poor trifles with which custom fills our days. But to be restlessly busy — to have and to seek no leisure, to accumulate what is equivocally called knowledge, to accelerate what is indefinitely called progress, to offer ourselves to the service of every master — is not necessarily to do our work. Nay, rather, this monotony of occupation excludes that exercise of thoughtful choice, that clear vision of the end, which gives the highest value to sacrifice. Then comes the Rest-day. The sharp contrast which it offers to other days constrains us in some degree to listen to its message. The closing of familiar books, the interruption of familiar engagements, the shut shops, the silent streets, the sense of freedom, the Church bells, almost force us to remember that man does not live by bread alone—to interrogate the past and the future—to examine our moral gains and hopes—to weigh the value of the knowledge which we are storing—to ponder the tendency and the end of the progress in which we share—to estimate the fresh responsibility which has been laid upon us by every fresh success—to add to every dream of hope or ambition the decisive question : 'If it be realised, what then ?'"   (P. 129.)

So the *power* of Sunday is set before us in words that go to the very heart of things ; and next, the responsibility for using and making known that power is made not less clear.

" It is on those of us who have leisure that the charge is laid to make clear to the world what the Sunday, the Christian Rest-day, is. If we seek only our own pleasure upon it, and do our own will ; if we render no offering of our ease and of our abundance ; if we make no burden lighter and think only how we ourselves may come before the face of God, on us must lie the sins of others who imitate our example in coarse and repulsive ways."   (P. 135.)

But as Christians we do not stop short at the thoughts of influence or responsibility, but pass on to the last and glorious vision of the true Sabbath *joy*.

" Happy are we then that we have still in our Sunday not only the opportunity but the invitation to 'rest awhile,' to lay ourselves open from week to week to the light and warmth of heaven, to gaze while the clouds break and angels are seen ascending and descending upon the Son of Man. Happy are we if we so listen to the call as to learn the meaning of our appointed service. Happy if, in these seasons of calm thought, we come to know that the failures and wants and sorrows and sins of men about us are occasions in which we, as disciples of Christ, may work the works of Him that sent us, in which we may work even as our Father works. . . ." (P. 137.)

"And whatever rules we may make for our own guidance, all will be summed up in this, that in every thought and word and wish on our 'Rest-day of heart' we shall bear ourselves as those who receive the day from Him with His blessing, and render it to Him for His hallowing. . . . So shall we win the manifold supports which our Rest-day offers for our necessities ; a truer perception of the claims, the methods, the possibilities of life ; an intelligent hope strong in the face of every evil ; a trust warmed by human sympathy. Without them, for most of at least, life will grow poorer and meaner and duller, closed within ever-narrowing limits till it becomes, as it were, a solitary struggle through a blinding storm, or a pitiful surrender to unreflecting self-indulgence." (P. 138.)

The responsibility, the power, and the joy are for all ; for all, too, is the final appeal :

"Oh, my friends, let us guard with the jealousy of love our Sunday, our Rest-day, our Sabbath,

K

for I cling to that first name, though it has been
dishonoured by material associations. . . . Our
Sunday, our Rest-day, has brought to us and to
our country more than we can know. . . . It
has kept us strong in the sense of allegiance to
an unseen power. . . . It has been to every
one of us, I am bold to say, at some time or
other, as an open gate of heaven, through which,
if only for a moment, we have caught a glimpse
of Him who has made it a promise, a beginning,
a rest, not *from* labour, but *for* labour." (P. 138.)

3. PRAYER

PERHAPS the most characteristic feature of Bishop Westcott's teaching about prayer is the ideal of fellowship, which is here also the pervading thought. To him prayer was not only or chiefly a means of getting what we want, but, first and foremost, the way to truest fellowship — with God first, and through God with men. By prayer, he taught, we learn first to know and then to do God's will— "which is our truest will." By prayer we are enabled to enter into that vital, heart-to-heart union with our fellow-men in which mutual help becomes a real thing.

" Fellowship in Intercession "—it was the subject of the Bishop's first address to his Diocese, the watchword which he chose for his work there ; it may almost be said to sum up his highest ideal of Christian prayer. At any rate, in those first words to his flock we shall find his teaching about prayer in its most impressive form.

Brethren, pray for us, was the burden of his appeal.

" *Brethren, pray for us*, even as I am pledged to bear you in my heart before God to my life's end." [1]

[1] *Incarnation and Common Life*, p. 16.

131

Even on the printed page, the words thrill with the earnestness with which the newly-made Bishop sought to make clear what the nature of that prayer should be.

" But what is the prayer for which I ask ? It is not the self-willed importunity of him who thinks that he shall be heard for his much speaking. It is not the opening to God of thoughts which His love has not anticipated. It is not the pleading of our personal wishes as isolated objects of divine favour. Nay, rather, it is the humblest, tenderest, most unquestioning expression of our dependence ; the confession of our wants and weaknesses, as we have felt them ; the firmest resolution to rest in God's will and to make His will our own ; the energy of a spiritual communion by which we realise our own well-being in the well-being of others ; the endeavour to quicken and chasten and hallow every prompting of duty by the light of Heaven.

" In this sense, brethren, *pray for us*. Such prayer corresponds with our Christian fellowship, with our present needs, with our divine assurance." [1]

Then came the thought of the universal *need* of fellowship.

" We are not, we cannot be, alone. In itself the fact is fitted to oppress us with the feeling of our powerlessness. But it can be transfigured. And to pray for one another is to

[1] *Incarnation and Common Life*, p. 5.

transfigure it. So to pray as feeling burdens which are not laid directly upon us, is to know that by God's most gracious dispensation we can lighten them. . . . So to pray as laying ourselves, our plans, our hopes, our acquirements, our opportunities, in the sight of God for His use, is to learn the lesson of life." [1]

The thought of fellowship, with Bishop Westcott, always leads on to the thought of work. This view of prayer as the highest source of power in practical endeavour comes out in all his writings; never more clearly, perhaps, than in the address on Foreign Missions quoted a few pages further on.[2] Never for a moment did he limit the power of prayer as applied to every need of human life; only he looked upon it always as the means for the fulfilment of the eternal will of God — "which is our truest will"—rather than of man's "chance desires." If worship was to him the hallowing of every effort, prayer was their inspiration, strength, and life.

"He read and worked in the very mind in which he prayed"—wrote one who had been his pupil—"and his prayer was of singular intensity."

Perhaps we can see something of the means by which he made it so in the advice which he gives to others in that strikingly practical little book, *Steps in the Christian Life.*

"A short habitual or deliberate pause before engaging in religious acts or entering sacred places, or in the midst of some great natural joy, or under the pressure of some disappoint-

---

[1] *Incarnation and Common Life*, p. 6.   [2] See p. 140.

ment, with the effort to feel God as actually listening to us, or waiting to receive us, or tempering for our use the gifts of His love, will bring to us a lively practical sense of that real atmosphere of the Divine by which we are surrounded . . .

". . . Our prayers, perhaps, are distracted, broken, we hardly know how, by wandering thoughts and blank vacancies of thought. In such a case an act of godly reverence in which we set before our minds the present and unspeakable majesty of God, as our Maker and Judge, who cannot but know, remember, try all—repeated, if need be, by an instantaneous thought as often as the attention flags—will assist us to realise that conscious communion with the unseen which is the essence of prayer. We must not rest till we feel that we are in the presence of a King. So the experience of the Psalmist will be our own : *I have set God always before me, therefore I shall not fall.*" [1]

[1] *Steps in the Christian Life*, p. 56 *et seq.*

VII

FOREIGN MISSIONS

FOREIGN MISSIONS

"The Church of Christ lives by the achievement of that which is impossible with men."—*Incarnation and Common Life*.

"It is His work, not ours; His strength, not ours; His command, not our choice."—*Ibid*.

OF Bishop's Westcott's devotion to the work of Foreign Missions, and of his share in that work, there is no need to speak. Both are witnessed abundantly in all that he has written and spoken on the subject, and, still more, in the long roll of workers from the Durham Diocese who heard through their Bishop's influence the call to go forth and win to Christ the nations that have not yet known His Name. What we want first of all to discover, in studying a man's writings for our personal help, is his characteristic teaching on any given subject—the special message which he has for those who look to him for guidance.

The main characteristic of Bishop Westcott's teaching on this subject of Foreign Missions, which lay so near his heart, is easily defined; for it is characteristic of his way of contemplating every region of thought or action.

It lay in considering nothing separately, as a matter by itself apart, but all in relation to the one

great subject which dominated his thoughts—the Incarnation of our Lord Jesus Christ.   Foreign Missions,
to the Bishop's mind, were not a separate sphere of
work, but a part of the self-same revelation of God's
purpose for the world, running through all history
from the earliest Scripture records, and summed up
in Christ.   Therefore in all his writings he entered
but little upon any detailed problems : but he was
for ever striving to make more clear the light in
which all these should be viewed.   Here, as in all
else, his call to those whom he taught was *Sursum
Corda*—lift up your hearts !   And the numbers are
beyond reckoning of those who have answered to
the call, and have learnt from it to look at Foreign
Missions in the light not of man's effort, but of
God's power and purpose, and so to gain a fresh
passion of zeal, a fresh force of devotion, and prayer,
and personal endeavour.

To look away from ourselves to God—to try and
discover not what we are able to effect, but what He
is willing and waiting to work through our means—
this is perhaps the duty to which the Bishop most
often calls us, in this as in every other sphere of
God's service.

As he writes in one place :

"To sum all then very briefly, the losing of
self in the supreme thought of God is the secret
of our power as Christians."[1]

And again, elsewhere :

"It is not a devout humility so much as an
unfaithful lukewarmness which draws a sharp

[1] *Christian Aspects of Life*, p. 50.

line between the Apostolic Missions and our own. Whatever difference does divide them, let us be sure of this, is due to man and not to God. . . . If there be a change in the efficacy of our appeals and our ministry, it is from ourselves. Not one promise made to the Church has been revoked. Not one gift has been annulled. Not one command has been withdrawn. 'Make disciples of all nations,' 'Receive the Holy Ghost,' 'I am with you all the days'—are still living words of a living Saviour, spoken once and spoken always. The slackness of our energy is alone able to hinder the progress of this triumph : the dimness of our vision is alone able to dull the effulgence of His glory." [1]

And in another address :

" Oh, my friends, it is the thought of self which puts aside or mars our noblest enterprises. It is the counting of our own resources which brings forgetfulness of the treasury of heaven. It is the straining of our natural vision which keeps the eyes of the soul closed. Our sight is blinded to the realities of the world. We are engrossed by the surface of things.[2]

" And when we cease to measure our endeavours by the standard of our own ability, room is opened for the action of God through us.[3]

" If we look for little, we find little. If we ask for much, we challenge a response of effort.[4]

---

[1] *Lessons from Work*, p. 201.
[2] *Incarnation and Common Life*, p. 221.
[3] *Ibid.* p. 220. [4] *Ibid.* p. 216.

" . . . I know something of the difficulties of the task, and I do not wish to dissemble or to disparage them : but the Church of Christ lives by the achievement of that] which is impossible with men." [1]

The work of Foreign Missions as a part of God's purpose, and therefore possible through Him—that was always, with the Bishop, the first thought ; and the next was the means by which the victory should be achieved.   This he summed up in the words of St. Paul, which he took as the text of one of his sermons on the subject : *Brethren, pray for us, that the Word of the Lord may run and be glorified.*

Prayer was the power he bade his hearers use and make their own ; in active effort he saw the means through which that power might find expression.

" Prayer is essentially active and expansive. If we pray for an object, we shall work for it also ; and we shall even without any set purpose make our interest in it felt.   If we pray for Missions in secret, we shall plead for Missions openly. . . . Zeal will kindle zeal, where before silence chilled it ; and devotion will pass into deed." [2]

" The treasury of prayer is open to all," he said in another place,[3] adding that Missions " are impossible, save through the prayers of the Church."

[1] *Incarnation and Common Life*, p. 220.
[2] *Lessons from Work*, p. 206.
[3] *Christian Aspects of Life*, p. 156.

And this prayer he longed to see offered not only in unwavering confidence, but also in childlike faith.

" We do not indeed care to inquire how prayer affects the will of God. It is enough for us to know that our God is a God who, seen under the conditions of human life, answers prayer. This is the testimony of the Mission Field. Our prayers then will carry there not only the deep and prevailing assurance of natural sympathy, but the pledge of divine help. It is not for us to prescribe—it is not for us to know the seasons which answer to the fitting accomplishment of the Father's purpose. We pray according to our most imperfect sight. We trust our prayers to the absolute love of God, sure at least of this, that no effort will be lost which is consecrated to Him, sure that the good seed which is watered with tears will hereafter bring gladness to the reaper's heart, sure that if we pray to Him, and as we pray to Him, the Lord of the Harvest will send forth his labourers ; some, as it must be, for the toil of patient waiting, and some for the toil of thankful ingathering, but all alike sobered and strengthened by the burden of His Cross, all alike crowned with the undying wreath of His victory." [1]

As he regarded the ultimate victory as certain in and through Christ, so the Bishop looked upon visible success and failure simply as different phases in human discipline.

[1] *Lessons from Work*, p. 209.

" It may be true, and I believe it is true "—he wrote—" that our chief successes, like the chief successes of the Apostles, have been confined to races who have no old book-religions : the fact, if it is so, imposes on us the obligation to study afresh our methods. Success and failure are given alike for our learning. Success and failure are in the hands of God. For us is the patience of unwearied labour, the willing acceptance of discipline, the watchful use of the opportunity." [1]

"Discouragement is the disenchantment of egoism" was another of his sayings. In an earlier sermon to the University of Cambridge, the Bishop has left us an example of this careful study of the lessons to be learned from both success and failure. He starts from a basis of absolute conviction that the power of the Incarnation is for all men, and that the root of all shortcomings lies in ourselves and not in the Gospel.

" The shaking of the Eastern peoples is, as we believe, the prelude to their offerings of devotion. The rapid spread of the Brahmo-Somaj and the energy of Mahommedan revival show that the strivings after the knowledge and the service of God are growing intenser with strange religions. And the fault must be ours if any who will to do the will of God, who contend passionately for a closer relationship with Him, who long to transfigure their life by their belief, do not find in the Gospel of the Incarnate Word the satisfaction of their longings, the realisation of their hope.

[1] *Lessons from Work*, p. 203.

The sentence stands written for our abiding comfort : In Him shall the Gentiles trust." [1]

From this general assertion of the responsibility of Foreign Missions, the Bishop goes on to consider in detail some causes of failure.   He notes in particular the four following, as serving specially to hinder work :

1. Undue insistence upon Western forms and traditions.
2. The too exclusive appeal to what is individual in the Christian Faith, at the expense of its wider social application.
3. The neglect of the important element of colonial life.
4. The tendency to denationalise races in Christianising them.

On the first of these points, he says, in the same sermon :

" Our missionary teaching hitherto has been, I say, for the most part too defined and traditional.   We have inherited a priceless treasure of elaborated doctrine, which represents the experience, the thought, the character of the West. We feel, more or less distinctly, how every detail of it is a pledge that Christianity answers to our special wants.   We know that it has grown with our growth, even if we are tempted to overlook the present energy of the Divine Spirit by whom it has been shaped.   Our first impulse, therefore, is to offer exactly that which

[1] *Religious Office of the Universities,* p. 28 *et seq.*

corresponds with our own position to men who are wholly different from us in history, in faculties, in circumstances of life. But in so doing we really contend, as far as lies in us, to impoverish the resources of humanity. We do dishonour to the infinite fulness of the Gospel. . . . If we could establish the loftiest type of Western Christianity in India as the paramount religion, and it is, I believe, wholly impossible to do so, our triumph would be in the end a loss to Christendom. We should lose the assurance of true victory which comes from the preservation and development of every power in the new citizens of the Kingdom of Christ. We should lose the integrity, the vitality, the infinity of our Faith, in the proud assertion of our own supremacy."

Next, on the danger of an exclusively individual teaching :

" There is a constant temptation, which we all feel in one way or other, to avoid the hardest forms of the problems which are offered to us. We are always looking for docile hearers, and for direct influence. After a first disappointment we are inclined to stigmatise as pride what may be after all the stern self-distrust of a sad heart. There is need of something more than the personal message of the individual preacher. And even when movement seems to be slowest, the power of Christ embodied in His Church will bring patience and sustain strength."

While the importance of using to the full the

existing power of our colonial life, suggests thoughts
which repay the deepest pondering :

> " Let the great questions of colonial life once
> take their place among us ; let them be con-
> sidered fairly in the light of our faith ; let it
> become habitual to us to regard all the interests
> and all the charges of duty as converging to one
> end ; and our missionaries will find that they
> have allies among our sons more powerful than
> themselves.

> " Our faith will be seen everywhere to be a life,
> and not a system—a life embracing every pro-
> duct of thought, and quickening every form of
> social existence."

The danger of destroying the nationality of
those whom we convert to Christianity is insisted
on with great decision.

> " Hitherto, as far as I know . . . our missionary
> teaching has failed also in this : it has been not
> only secondary and individual—it has been also
> denationalising.   It is very difficult for us to
> appreciate the overpowering effect of a dominant
> class in enforcing their own beliefs.   It is even
> more difficult to apprehend the relative shape
> which these beliefs assume in the minds of alien
> races. . . . If we are to proclaim in its fulness a
> Gospel which is universal and not Western, we
> must keep ourselves and our modes of thought
> studiously in the background.   We must aim at
> something far greater than collecting scattered
> congregations round English clergy who may

reflect to our eye faint and imperfect images
of ourselves. We must watch carefully lest
Christianity should be regarded simply as the
religion of the stronger or the wiser. We must
take to heart the lessons of the first age, lest we
unconsciously repeat the fatal mistake of the
early Judaisers, and offer as permanent that
which is accidental and transitory. We must
adopt every mode of influence which can be
hallowed to the service of the Faith, the asceticism,
the endurance, the learning which are indigenous
to the country. We must follow the religious
instincts and satisfy the religious wants of Hindu
and Mohammedan through the experience of
men from among themselves. We can in some
degree, as the Spirit helps us, teach the teachers,
but we cannot teach the people."

But even in pointing out the difficulties and
dangers of the work, the Bishop never lost sight of
the power by which all could be overcome. The
conclusion of the sermon is characteristic.

"The need is urgent, but it is inspiring. The
time is short, but spiritual progress is not gauged
by temporal measures. The work is arduous,
but our strength is the strength of the Incarnation.

"The day is at hand: and therefore a fresh
glory of Christ shall follow our time of waiting:
in Him shall the nations trust: and their hope
shall not be unaccomplished."

This, then, is the special lesson which Bishop

Westcott has to teach us on Foreign Missions, as on
every other subject that he touched—to see Christ
in all things, and ourselves, in a most real and
practical sense, "in Christ."   Missions were to him
always an endeavour "to proclaim Him in Whom
we are, Him Whose perfect obedience has made our
obedience possible." [1]

> "We proclaim not merely a system of theology,
> not an abstract idea, but a 'Person' loving and
> to be loved, speaking and to be spoken to—a
> Saviour, Priest, and King, present with us all the
> days.   Our message"—he adds in words that
> speak straight to the soul—"is a test of what
> the Gospel is to us.   We cannot in the case of
> races among whom the historic sense is un-
> developed, at once appeal to the events of the
> Passion and Resurrection as past facts of unique
> significance, but we can point them to the present
> effects of the love and power which those events
> revealed and still communicate.   We can make
> clear what they are to us ; we can make clear
> how they fill us with tenderness and courage ;
> we can make clear that we believe and act as
> believing that Christ not only died and ascended
> for the most desolate, but that He lives for them
> now, that He bears them in His heart on His
> Father's throne, that He is as near to them as
> He is to us.   The living, loving, reigning Christ,
> Son of Man, and Son of God, uniting in Himself
> earth and heaven, time and eternity,—this is the
> Gospel which we are charged to publish." [2]

[1] *Christian Aspects of Life*, p. 169.   [2] *Ibid.* p. 170.

NOTE

Christian Aspects of Life contains two of the Bishop's addresses on Foreign Missions ; *The Incarnation and Common Life*, *Words of Faith and Hope*, and *Lessons from Work* each contain one.

Lessons from Work gives also, in the Appendix, the correspondence between the Bishop and his junior clergy, on Foreign Service. This should be read by all who wish to get a full idea of the Bishop's own views on the subject, and of his influence.

For deeper study, readers are referred to the *Gospel of Life*, a book difficult to master, but well worth the effort. A brief outline of it, reprinted from the *Church Reading Magazine*, is given in the Appendix to the present volume.

VIII

PRACTICAL PROBLEMS

PRACTICAL PROBLEMS

" The most far-reaching arguments, the highest motives, are the most practical. No self-centred considerations will shield a man in temptation. But the vision of Christ will, for He will support the effort which is made in acknowledgment of a duty which is owed to Him."—*Incarnation and Common Life.*

" The conception which we form of our duty is of more importance than our first most imperfect performance."—*Ibid.*

" I have only indicated principles, but they are luminous for our guidance. If they are accepted they are capable of transforming our whole life, little by little, to a divine pattern."—*Ibid.*

THESE few sentences express the spirit in which Bishop Westcott faced the most practical problems as well as the deepest spiritual needs of life. He teaches here the same lesson precisely that he teaches about the Scriptures—*how to look at them.* The conditions of social questions change so rapidly that for their detailed study we must always turn to the writers of the present moment. But for the unchanging principles which should guide that study, Bishop Westcott can help us, with a help that is never out of date. For he shows us how to look through and beyond the shifting surface of practical problems, to discern their real meaning, and God's will for us as shown through them : and this lesson is the same for all.

It is worked out, perhaps, the most fully in the

Bishop's great charge on social problems, which he issued under the characteristic title, " The Incarnation a Revelation of Human Duties." [1]

" The Incarnation,"—he wrote, in one of the opening sentences,—" in proportion as we give a distinct meaning to the truth, must become to us a revelation of human duties, and it is in this light I invite you to regard it."

To bring the light of God in Christ to bear upon every problem—this was his special call to us.

> "It is, then, of vital importance "—he says a few pages later—" that we . . . should approach social problems from a Christian point of sight. If we believe in the Fall, and the Redemption, and the Mission of the Spirit, the belief, so far as the belief is realised, must affect our judgments, our actions, our hopes.
>
> " . . . All man and all being, therefore, come within the range of the Christian's hope ; and our most frequent prayer—*Thy kingdom come*—reminds us that the Lord presents earth as the scene of our consummation. . . . To us, also, when we are lost in vain speculations on the mysteries of the divine working, the words come : *Why stand ye gazing up into heaven ?* (Acts i. 11).
>
> " We need this awakening summons to that which we may think secular work. . . . For us each amelioration of man's circumstances is the translation of a fragment of our Creed into action, and not the self-shaped effort of a kindly nature.   It answers, as we believe, to the will

[1] *Incarnation and Common Life*, pp. 41-106.

of God ; and the faith which quickened the purpose is sufficient to accomplish it.

" . . . The Christian Faith covers all life—the personal life, the life of the citizen, the life of the man.   Each least and nearest interest gains in intensity as a wider interest is acknowledged. As Christians, therefore, we are bound ourselves to study, and, as far as we may be able, to lead others to study the Christian ideal of our personal relations, of our class relations, of our national relations ; and then to determine the next step which we can take in each direction towards it."

This was the line of thought which the Bishop endeavoured in this charge to work out in relation to some of the most pressing problems of the day. For the true and lasting solution of those problems —of all alike—he recognised two needs above all others : the need of *fellowship*, and the need of *service*.

" It is impossible "—he insisted—" for any one to confine the effects of what he does, or leaves undone, to himself alone.   If he withdraws himself into a desert, and spends his years in completest isolation, he defrauds his fellow-men of the fruits of the large heritage which he has received from the past.   In the stir of action every man at every moment influences others, consciously or unconsciously, limiting and moulding them, scattering seeds of thought and deed which will be fruitful of good or evil while time lasts.   If the solitary ascetic is to justify himself he must show—and there are

times perhaps when this would be possible—
that his impressive protest against the spirit of
the age is worth the cost at which it is made.
If the man of affairs is to justify his life of
restless enterprise, he must not appeal to
material results, but to the signs of character
strengthened and purified."

And then—always the thought in which his
mind found rest after its loftiest flights—" the responsibility of living might well appal us by its
immeasurable issues, but as children we can rest
gladly in our Father's will."

The practical application of this thought of
fellowship is clearly shown, and is of the deepest
value.

> "The essence of sin lies in selfishness—self-
> assertion. . . . Brought to this test the great
> questions of temperance and purity can be
> dealt with effectually. The virtues are positive
> and not negative. They are not personal but
> social. Any indulgence which lessens our own
> efficiency or brings injury on another is sinful. . . .
>
> ". . . False-dealing in trade and gambling
> can, I believe, only be overcome by the applica-
> tion of the same truth. They are offences
> against our fellowship in Christ. We must
> present them in this light. Nor will any one
> think that such a view is exaggerated who has
> reflected on the reason which St. Paul gives for
> truthfulness. *Speak ye truth*, he writes, *each
> one with his neighbour, because we are members
> one of another.*" (Eph. iv. 25).

The reminder which follows is one which we all need :

> " I touch on these most obvious points, for I think that we commonly shrink from bringing the great truths of our Faith to bear on the trials and duties of every day. Yet commonplace events make up the staple of our lives. Our ordinary occupations must form nine-tenths of our service,—our service to God and to man,—and if the power of our Faith is to be felt, we require not only private devotion, but open confession (1 John iv. 3). . . . We have no difficulty in looking to our day's work as it is given to us day by day, as something to be done for God's glory and man's welfare in our Father's presence and through His help."

Then, with one of those flashes of insight which reveal the difference between the Christian and the worldly view of life :

> " So it is with the bulk of our middle class. It is otherwise with the very rich and with the very poor. In this respect extremes meet, and it is hard to say whether superfluity or penury is more unfavourable to the realisation of the true ideal of life. On the one side the pressure of conventional engagements and pleasures tends to crowd out the thought of service ; on the other side the conditions of labour are such as to obscure the truth that this labour may be the service of a son."

The simple standard of *service*—service to God

and man—was the only one by which the Bishop, as a Christian, could measure wealth. Great wealth meant, in his view, "the opportunity for great self-denials."

" Differences of culture, or place, or wealth, are opportunities for characteristic service," he urged elsewhere.

And again, in another address :

" Great possessions may become great blessings to him who matches them with great counsels. And on every side there is now sore need of the utmost help of such as have most. Not for themselves, but for those who have no reserve, men hold the accumulated fruits of earlier industry. Not for themselves, but for those who are bound by daily toil, they hold the perilous gift of leisure. Not for themselves, but for those who trust the culture which they have not, they hold the treasures of learning and art. Not for themselves, but for those who respond to generous sympathy, they hold the great traditions of birth and rank. We may misapply, or waste, or neglect our resources, whatever they are : we may leave our work unfulfilled. But there is a benediction prepared for the discipline of anxious cares. If we fail to win it, our failure will come not from the largeness of the divine bounty, but because in the contemplation of our endowments we neglected to act in the name of the Lord Jesus." [1]

[1] *Incarnation and Common Life*, p. 132.

The accumulated fruits of earlier industry—such was the unvarying light in which the Bishop looked upon inherited riches.

"Resources which we inherit, in intellect or wealth"—he wrote elsewhere—"are the opportunities of larger service. It is no less ignoble to live idly on the gifts of the past, than to live idly on the alms of our contemporaries."[1]

And again, in yet another place :

"Can any outward poverty compare with this inner poverty which touches not the circumstances of life, but the powers of life, which leaves the wealthiest beggared in thought in the midst of his splendour, and the wisest destitute of sympathy in the midst of his intellectual triumphs ? Oh, brethren, when once we feel what life is, we feel then, and not till then, what poverty is, manifold as the regions of life."[2]

This same standard of service by which the Bishop measured wealth he also applied to every kind of luxury. Perhaps no more complete or searching test of luxury could be devised than that contained in a single sentence :

"That, therefore, is a culpable luxury for an individual which costs more either in money or time, or vital energy, than it contributes to his power of service."[3]

[1] *Incarnation and Common Life*, p. 30.
[2] *Ibid.* p. 300.   [3] *Ibid.* p. 134.

That was the central thought, worked out more fully in other passages :

> " A life spent in the pursuit of enjoyment cannot justly claim to be a human, still less a Christian life. Every exceptional indulgence in amusement or living which we admit, every use which we make of money or leisure for rest, for travel, for the accumulation of works of art or literature, must satisfy two tests before it can be approved by an awakened conscience. It must be found to contribute directly or indirectly its full value to the efficiency of our work ; and it must not be such as to cause even the weak to offend by a perilous example." [1]

And again :

> " We can habitually ask ourselves whether this or that exceptional indulgence is required for the efficiency of our service, and press the question upon others. . . . We can help those who look only on the surface of things to understand something of the burden of great possessions. We can show that we wish to use all whereby God has made us to differ from others, not for the assertion of our superiority but for better service, *not saying that aught of the things which we possess is our own.*" [2]

In words such as these, hard as they are to grasp in their full meaning — harder still to carry into practice — we have offered to us the true touchstone for all the aims and ambitions and desires that crowd

[1] *Incarnation and Common Life*, p. 134.   [2] *Ibid.* p. 62.

our lives.   In considering these the Bishop gives
us yet another thought to ponder, in his estimate of
success.   The visible and immediate success in
which we so often see the longed-for crown of our
efforts was to him rather a peril than a prize.

> " Success, though it must of necessity be in-
> complete, tends to satisfy us.   It leads us to
> substitute a part for the whole, to acquiesce in
> the less which we have gained, and to forget the
> greater at which we aimed — perhaps to rest
> contented with material profit, and to lose the
> spiritual aspirations which have been, indeed,
> the very soul of our efforts." [1]

Does such a view strike us as visionary, impracticable, vague—a counsel of perfection too high
to be carried out in our everyday life of struggle and
stress ?   If so, we can learn from Bishop Westcott's
own words by what means he made them, what
they were to himself, the rule of every day.

> " I do wish"—was his appeal on the occasion
> of his own enthronement—" speaking, as I believe
> in the spirit of the great office in which I desire
> to sink myself, to claim the whole of life, every
> human interest, every joy and every sorrow,
> every noble aspiration and every true thought,
> as falling within the domain of our Faith." [2]

And again, in another place :

> " The babble of innumerable voices drowns the
> name of the Lord Jesus when it is sounded in

---

[1] *Incarnation and Common Life*, p. 241.   [2] *Ibid*. p. 10.

our ears.   None the less life, with all it brings,
is given us that we may receive and reflect that
glory, that we may welcome and proclaim that
name. . . . So may we, turning our Faith into
act, *do all things for the glory of God. . . .*" [1]

And yet again, on the subject this time not of
the employment of wealth, but of co-operation in
commerce :

"I have dared to express great aspirations,
because I believe more confidently as the years
go on that men are moved by lofty motives.
For me, co-operation rests upon my Faith.   It
is the active expression, in terms of our present
English life, of the articles of my Creed."

With such passages as these before us, who will
dare to say that Bishop Westcott's views, or his
teaching, were "indefinite," "unpractical," or "vague"?
Quotations might be multiplied indefinitely, but
those already given are enough to show the spirit in
which he confronted social questions ; and readers
who wish for fuller details will do well to seek them
for themselves in the writings already referred to,
and in the others which touch upon these subjects.
And it is safe to say that no one has tried to bring
these views—lofty and ideal as they are—to bear
upon the actual problems and temptations of every
day, without finding life grow, in some degree at
least, better worth living.

The Incarnation and Common Life, from which
all the above passages are taken, is the book which

[1] *Incarnation and Common Life*, 136.

contains the largest number of the Bishop's writings upon social subjects. *Christian Aspects of Life* includes three addresses, delivered to the Christian Social Union, and *Lessons from Work* two more of these. These five, together with two others not included in any other collection, are reprinted in the small and inexpensive volume of *Christian Social Union Addresses*.

Words of Faith and Hope gives two addresses on social problems : one on " Labour Co-operation," and one—Bishop Westcott's last public utterance in his cathedral—to the Durham miners, on " The Sovereign Motive." In this the Bishop, with the intention at the moment only of closing his own share in these annual addresses to the miners, unconsciously closed and summed up his life-work in the words with which he bade his hearers farewell :

" Therefore, since it is not likely that I shall ever address you here again, I have sought to tell you what I have found in a long and laborious life to be the most prevailing power to sustain right endeavour, however imperfectly I have yielded myself to it ; even the love of Christ : to tell you what I know to be the secret of a noble life, even glad obedience to His will. I have given you a watchword which is fitted to be the inspiration, the test and the support of untiring service to God and man : *the love of Christ constraineth us.*" [1]

The words were spoken on 20th July 1901, and seven days later Bishop Westcott passed from his

[1] *Words of Faith and Hope.*

M

labours on earth to the unseen life which had always been so near to him. To those of us who have learnt to treasure his teaching as one of the best inspirations of our lives, this parting "watchword" rings home with solemn and most touching force.

IX

THOUGHTS ON MANY SUBJECTS

THOUGHTS ON MANY SUBJECTS

" Great thoughts are more than thoughts. They are witnesses to us of that greater life to which I have pointed. . . . They are not of our creation. They are the gift of God, and man can take them to himself and live by them, because he was made in God's image."— *Incarnation and Common Life*.

" Only let those of us who have caught some distant glimpse of the beauty of creation as the thought of God, and of the obligation of labour as the lot of man, tell courageously what we have seen and known. All who share our nature are capable of our highest visions, and awakened reverence will do her perfect work.—*Ibid*.

BESIDES the definite and connected teaching of any great master, there are always flashes of insight, new gleams of light upon old truths, to be met with, scattered through his writings. The value of these is of course different for every different reader, depending as it does upon the response evoked by individual needs. Some thoughts, however, are of wider application than others, and I have tried to gather here a few of these from Bishop Westcott's works. Readers who will take the trouble to carry on the search for themselves, will be rewarded with a far richer harvest.

On Suffering

Here we have the subject of all others which appeals to our restless, troubled, self-torturing human hearts. Those to whom the problem of suffering has not yet come home in any personal guise, will doubtless pass by these thoughts as devoid of meaning; but such readers will be very few. Upon most of us, when we have passed our childhood, if not before, suffering has forced itself as a dread reality, in the form of either pain, or loss, or the long-drawn anguish of unfulfilled desires. And most of us, at one time or another, have fiercely or sadly questioned that dark, stern mystery.

Over and over again in his writings Bishop Westcott has sought to answer these questionings; or rather, to show where the answer to them may be found, where he himself sought it, in the vision of what lies beyond the veil of human life and human tears. Let those who have suffered take and try his thoughts, applying them to their own hearts' needs.

"Dimly, feebly, imperfectly, we can see . . . how Christ, Himself perfected through suffering, has made known to us, once for all, the meaning and the value of suffering; how He has interpreted it as a divine discipline, the provision of a Father's love; how He has left us to realise '*in Him*,' little by little, the virtue of His work; *to fill up on our part*, in the language of St. Paul, *that which is lacking of the afflictions of Christ* in our own sufferings, not as if His work were incomplete or our efforts meritorious, but as being living members of His Body, through which He is pleased to manifest that which He has wrought for men." [1]

[1] *Christus Consummator*, p. 27.

Again he wrote, on those same words of St. Paul's :

"In these wonderful words a glimpse is opened to us of another aspect of the blessing of sorrows in Christ. They are fertile, not only for ourselves, but for others. That unity of life which brings to us the efficacy of Christ's work, carries our work beyond us. . . . He never sought suffering for its own sake. He never shrank from it when it was for the fulfilment of His Father's will. It was an instrument of conquest, a means of service. So it must be with us. And who would wish one pang to be removed which serves in any way to hasten the end of Christ's victory? We know all too well our unworthiness and weakness, yet all mercy and strength follow us. We fail, and our High Priest is ready *to make propitiation for our sins* ; we faint, and He places within our reach grace to help in time of need." [1]

Then again comes the same thought, growing ever clearer :

"The way of the Lord is the way of His servants. He enlightened the path which they must tread, and showed its end. And so it is that whenever the example of Christ is offered to us in Scripture for our imitation, it is His example in suffering. So far, in His strength, we can follow Him, learning obedience as He learned it, bringing our wills into conformity

[1] *Victory of the Cross*, p. 89.

with the Father's will, and thereby attaining to
a wider view of His counsel in which we can
find rest and joy. . . .

" Responsive love transfigures that which it
bears. Pain loses its sting when it is mastered
by a stronger passion. The true secret of happi-
ness is not to escape toil and affliction, but to
meet them with the faith that through them
we can even now reflect the image of our Lord
and be transformed into His likeness." [1]

High thoughts they are ; too high for us to grasp,
we may be tempted to think, when the agony is very
keen. And yet the very effort to lift our thoughts
away from self is in itself a help ; and as we
make it, we gain at least some gleams of light—
some vision of a far-off possibility of comfort—
through and beyond the storms, from these next
words of confidence.

" The power of love is not limited by its personal effects. It goes out upon others with a
healing virtue. . . . Love kindles love ; and, in
the world as we see it, suffering feeds the purifying flame. Was I not right, then, when I said
that the thought of Christ, perfected through
suffering, does indeed bring light into the darkest
places of the earth? In that light, suffering, if
I may so speak, appears as the fuel of love.
Up to a certain point we can clearly perceive
how the vicissitudes, the sadnesses, the trials of
life, become the springs of its tenderness, and
strength, and beauty . . . how the truest joys

1 *Christus Consummator*, p. 28.

which we have experienced have come when we have had grace to enter most fully into a sorrow not our own. And even where sight fails, the virtue of the Lord's life, made perfect through suffering, guides us still." [1]

" Every new birth is through sorrow. The last gift of Christ to His disciples before the Passion was the gift of His peace, not the peace of a still calm untroubled by conflicts, but the peace which reigns supreme through the sorest trials, the sharpest agonies, the fiercest assaults, because it rests on the consciousness of an eternal son-ship. We have no promise that we shall be free from suffering : it is enough that no suffer-ing shall be fruitless which is seen in the issue of the Father's will." [2]

Such are the thoughts which give us courage to face our share of suffering, if not without shrinking, at least without despair ; and the " conclusion of the whole matter " is summed up in a single sentence.

" Gain through apparent loss ; victory through momentary defeat ; the energy of a new life through pangs of travail,—such has ever been the law of spiritual progress." [3]

Anxiety and Loss

In a sense, these come under the head of suffer-ing, and yet they are a kind of suffering apart by

---

[1] *Christus Consummator*, p. 29.
[2] *Victory of the Cross*, p. 88.
[3] *Christus Consummator*, p. 3.

themselves. For the bitterness of loss, and the long strain of anxiety, are wholly different in their nature from the passionate fever of unfulfilled desires.

To the heart-breaking questions which confront the mourner and the watcher, Bishop Westcott had also an answer to suggest—the answer in which he himself had found the secret of his strong serenity.

> " The times when I have been most anxious have been just those when I have felt most the unseen greatness of life. Power has seemed to flow in, not thought of before. We have come already, though for the most part our eyes are holden, to innumerable hosts of ministering spirits, and to God Himself. There can be no loss of that which is most precious. . . ." [1]

" *There can be no loss of that which is most precious* "—words to be graven deeply into every heart that loves.

It is the same thought, further worked out, in the next passage, written about the same great blow to earthly hopes.[2]

> " Such events reveal the nature of life. They force us to feel that what we see is only a sign of that which *is*. . . . Life is more than the present forms of life, and must be effective according to its nature when it passes out of sight. We tremble when we say it, yet earthly loss, even the most overwhelming, is not, if we

---

[1] *Life of Bishop Westcott*, vol. ii. p. 20.
[2] The illness and death of his son-in-law.

hold our faith, loss in the eternal light. We may perhaps see how, when the Lord said 'It is expedient for you that I go away,' He interpreted for us our separations. He went away not to leave, but to be nearer to His people." [1]

This same thought of gain through apparent loss, and closer union through seeming separation, was the subject of his first public utterance as Bishop in his own diocese. Speaking on the occasion of his own enthronement, his thoughts turned naturally to his predecessor, the beloved fellow-worker of so many years, whose friendship, as he said elsewhere, did not seem " so much to have been interrupted as to have been consecrated for evermore." [2] And the first lesson that he taught his people is one that we all need to learn : the lesson of looking at the past, as well as at the present and future, in the light of the unseen.

" We cannot but look back to the 15th of May, eleven years ago, when, speaking in this place, my predecessor laid open the secret of his life and work, the reverent fixing of his soul's eye upon the vision of the eternal presence—a vision of righteousness, and grace, and glory, which is for the believer a vision of purification and strength. And now, as we humbly hope, for him the vision of faith has become the vision of experience, and he 'sees the face' of Him on whom he trusted. . . .

[1] *Life of Bishop Westcott,* vol. ii. p. 20.
[2] *From Strength to Strength,* p. 43.

" . . . We cannot but look back, and, if at first we are touched with natural sorrow in the retrospect, sorrow is soon turned into hope. We perceive, even with our feeble powers, that beneath all these vicissitudes one unchanging counsel of love goes forward to its accomplishment ; that work and rest, effort and self-surrender, the stress of conflict and the silence of the grave, are facts of the one life whereby alone we live. What is lost to the eye rises transfigured in the soul, and we come to know that when the Lord said, ' It is expedient for you that I go away,' He revealed a divine law, by which each bereavement, each apparent loss, becomes through His grace the source of new spiritual blessing." [1]

It was in the same strain that Bishop Westcott spoke, in the same place, on the death of another of his lifelong friends, Archbishop Benson.

" Such losses, indeed, bring a corresponding gain. They give a human reality to the unseen world. Those on whom we look no longer are, in some sense, felt to be more continuously near than when they moved among us under the conditions of earth ; and their spiritual presence supplies a living and intelligible form to the Communion of Saints, through which we enter on the powers of the eternal life." [2]

[1] *Incarnation and Common Life*, p. 3 *et seq.*
[2] *Life of Bishop Westcott*, vol. ii. p. 209.

Sympathy

The thought of sympathy follows naturally upon the thought of suffering, for "love can lighten the weight of suffering which it cannot remove: it can transform what it cannot destroy."[1]

"Taught in this great school of domestic national, human fellowship, we are coming to understand, as we could not do before, that to noble and pure souls some imperfect yet real power of restoration is given, proportioned to their knowledge and their sympathy and their holiness, to their capacity for entering into the hearts of the ignorant, the weak and the erring, and for calling out in them the response of penitent devotion: to understand that in the unity of the body it is possible for one member to take away the infirmity and disease of another by taking them to himself.

". . . We are coming to understand, in a word, what is the true meaning of that phrase, ' vicarious suffering,' which has brought at other times sad perplexity to anxious minds ; how it excludes everything that is arbitrary, fictitious, unnatural, external in human relationships ; how it expresses the highest energy of love which takes a friend's sorrows into the loving heart and transfigures them, satisfying every claim of righteousness, justifying every instinct of hope, quickening the spirit of self-surrender, offering within the sphere

[1] *Christus Consummator*, p. 121.

of common life a faint image of forgiveness, of redemption, of reconciliation." [1]

Such thoughts as these open undreamed-of possibilities of comfort, when once we have learnt to grasp as a reality the conviction underlying them all, that " the unseen must be the larger part of life." [2]

On this conviction also there are some of the Bishop's words that speak to every heart.

The Power of the Unseen

". . . It is this conviction which we need above all to make our own. We need to see life as God made it, to bring to light its spiritual side, to show it in connection with the unseen. That which is poor and sordid and trivial is changed when the light of heaven falls upon it. Such a blessing, the blessing of Christ, Born, Crucified, Risen, Ascended, is as universal as the sunshine if we will give it entrance, if we will find it entrance. And to give the entrance, to find the entrance, is our work—our work by the grace of God for ourselves and for others, as those who *walk by faith, not by sight*.[3]

" What we see is not all : what we see is not even the dim image of that which *is*. The life which we feel, the life which we share, is more than the earthly materials by which it is at present sustained, more than the earthly vestures through which it is at present manifested. That

---

[1] *Christus Consummator*, p. 122 *et seq.*

[2] *Life of Bishop Westcott*, vol. ii. p. 321.

[3] *Incarnation and Common Life*, p. 372.

is not most real which can be touched and
measured, but that which struggles, as it were, to
find imperfect expression through the veils of
sense. . . .

". . . Yes, the unseen and the eternal is for all
of us who confess Christ come, Christ coming in
flesh, the ruling thought of life. . . ."[1]

Such convictions, Bishop Westcott taught, are
most intensely practical, for "they encourage us to
bring our ordinary thoughts and feelings into the
light of our eternal destiny."[2]

Difficulties in the Way of realising the Unseen

Of these we all are conscious; the more keenly,
very often, the more we try to overcome them.
Bishop Westcott recognised them fully, and has
shown us how to trace them to their source.

"Every one feels, and in word deplores, the
hurry of modern life. The days are crowded
with engagements; and we seek to fill with
excitement whatever intervals of leisure may
be left to us. We are afraid to be alone, to be
silent, to be ourselves. 'The world is too much
with us.' Under the pressure of constant occupation we borrow our opinions, our arguments,
our standards, our rules of conduct. We have
no time, so we think, to place ourselves, calm
and receptive, in the presence of the unseen
realities which lie behind the transitory phenomena of life. We shrink from the solitude in

[1] *Christus Consummator*, p. 56 *et seq.*   [2] *Ibid.* p. 60.

which God speaks. And still our faculties, our opportunities, our difficulties, our temptations, are ours alone. The responsibility of dealing with them is ours. We cannot live our proper life either at random or by tradition. All alike need to look to the eternal in quiet moments with the eyes of their heart, in order that they may see what their life is. And all can command the inspiring vision.

"Time is no measure of spiritual effort, or of spiritual experience. The discipline and the blessing of retirement can, if it must be so, be found in the crowd. But there are few of us who are unable to command brief occasions when we may listen in the still church . . . or under the clear sky, for voices which the waiting soul will not fail to hear.

". . . Life is not easy. It appears to be a divine law that the difficulty of a duty increases with its importance. The sense of the importance of the issue, when it is once realised, sustains the vigour of the endeavour. But we must see our own duty first for ourselves, as in the presence of God, and then seek the power to fulfil it. . . . What we require to know is not the divine will generally, but the divine will for us. This knowledge will not be gained all at once. Each attainment brings the promise of a larger view. The question, What is life for us? will receive an answer always new and always old. Life is in every part an offering to God, and to men in Him." [1]

[1] *Incarnation and Common Life*, p. 395 *et seq.*

Labour

The part which Bishop Westcott took in dealing
with the labour problems of the day was too important, and his thoughts on the subject too far-
reaching, to be adequately represented by a few
quotations. All that these can do is to show the
lines which he followed here, as in every other region
of life and thought. Perhaps the most complete
expression, in a brief form, of his views upon the
problems of labour in the present day is to be found
in his charge on the " Incarnation as a Revelation of
Human Duties." [1]

" A man's daily labour is the chief element in
determining his character. It is by this he
serves and by this he grows. It is substantially
his life, to be begun and ended, day by day, in
the name of God. Thus the labour question is
in the fullest sense a religious question. The
workman is commonly said to offer his work in
the market as a commodity. In fact, he offers
himself. If, then, the conditions of labour are
not such as to make a true human life possible
for the labourer, if he receives as the price of his
toil a mutilated and impoverished manhood, there
can be no lasting peace : there can be no prevailing Christian faith.[2]

" Worship is a very small fragment of devotion.
The Christian does not offer to God part of his
life or of his endowments in order that he may
be at liberty to use the rest according to his

[1] *Incarnation and Common Life*, p. 41 *et seq.*   [2] *Ibid.* p. 64.

N

own caprice. All life, all endowments, are equally owed to our Lord, and equally claimed by Him. Every human office in every part is holy.[1]

" And our ordinary work, let us remember, is the staple of our lives. It does not, as we too commonly suppose, furnish the means of living : it is living. And there is no delight comparable to the delight which comes from a sense of doing one's best in one's common duty.[2]

" . . . The days of most of us are filled by routine, but routine may be elevated if we look through it and beyond it to a great ideal. The ideal, if it is cherished, becomes an inspiration, and leads us through failures and sadnesses to forget ourselves and rest only in God." [3]

The Need for the Open Confession of our Faith

This need, already touched on in the foregoing passage, was so constantly and so closely present to Bishop Westcott's mind, that thoughts on the subject will be found recurring again and again throughout his writings. In the following words it found expression with striking force and clearness.

" The review of a day or of a week may well lead us to ask, not without sad misgivings, ' How would men know that we are Christians ? ' Is there anything in our tone, or temper, or aims, or conduct, which constrains those who do not

[1] *Incarnation and Common Life*, p. 128.
[2] *Ibid*. p. 250.   [3] *Ibid*. p. 128.

share our Faith to recognise that it is a power over us and in us? If it has not given us new convictions as to our relations to our fellow-men, as to the use of our possessions—moral, intellectual, material—can we be said to really hold it? If it exercises no restraint, if it supplies no guidance, if it kindles no aspirations, if it supports no endurance, if it brings no strength, what does it mean for us?

"We cannot be Christians in fragments. Christianity finds expression in a Christian life, and not simply in Christian acts. There is an infinite difference between failure and acquiescence in failure. It is not humility, but indolence, which accepts a low standard. If we deliberately live below our calling, it is sin. We shrink instinctively from hypocrisy: but it is no less hypocrisy to dissemble the good desires by which we are possessed, than to affect devotion which we do not feel. Our Faith—we must dare to say it, with whatever shame it may be—lays upon us great obligations, and offers great resources. The Lord says to us, if we are His disciples, '*Ye are the light of the world; ye are the salt of the earth.*' Such a commission constrains us to inquire importunately till our souls return some answer, What have we done, what are we doing . . . to bring home to men the Gospel of the Risen Christ, by which things transitory and corruptible are invested with an eternal glory?"[1]

"There is, I think, nothing sadder in the world than the waste of Christian influence.

[1] *Incarnation and Common Life*, p. 396.

From one cause or another, we shrink from the responsibility of avowing our deepest convictions. . . . By so doing, we wrong our friends. We leave unspoken the word which might have cheered, or guided, or turned them. . . . No one, I fancy, has ever ventured to cast aside his religious reserve without meeting with sympathy for which he had not looked, and gaining courage from the sense of spiritual fellowship." [1]

" We think of ourselves, and our hearts fail us. We look round and find no help adequate to our needs. We do not — this is the secret of every failure—*believe in the Holy Ghost.* Our controversies, our perplexities, our restless searchings in the past, our timorousness, all combine to condemn us of want of faith in a living, acting, speaking God. . . . ' Heaven lies about us' still, and as we turn heavenward light falls on our darkness, and weakness becomes strength. This then is the truth which I commend above all others to the patient, resolute, open contemplation of all who desire to fulfil the vows of their baptism,—the Presence among us of a living Spirit. He is, we profess, 'the Lord, the Giver of Life'; and He is this not in some remote sphere but here and now. Do we then, from day to day, in our work and in our rest, look to Him, offer ourselves to Him, listen for His voice, withdraw nothing from His purifying influence, and confide in complete self-surrender upon His unfailing grace?" [2]

[1] *Christian Life*, p. 72.
[2] *Incarnation and Common Life*, p. 397.

The power of self-surrender was one on which Bishop Westcott laid unwearied stress.

> "Self-surrender is accompanied by transformation. God quickens and transfigures by illuminating. . . Self-surrender, transformation, service: this is what Christ asked for us: this is what, by His intercession, He places within our reach. No one can deny our need of the blessing; no one can deny its power." [1]

No one, certainly, who has seen that power displayed in the Bishop's own life of widespread influence and deepest consecration.

Christian Service

"Service is a necessary element in the fulness of Christian life."

So Bishop Westcott taught repeatedly, and has added here and there practical suggestions as to the way in which that service can be offered.

Some of the simplest and most direct of these are contained in an address to the Church people of Sunderland.

> ". . . But then, many may say—many here are saying now—'I have so little power; so little time; so few and fleeting opportunities,—that the little I can bring would make no difference to the final result.' But, my friends, in such questions as these there is no consideration of great and little. What God requires of us is

[1] *Incarnation and Common Life*, pp. 182, 187.

simply what we have to offer—what we are. He requires no more, but He requires no less. And we are very poor judges in spiritual things of what is great and what is little. Our joy is to remember that God has tempered the whole body together, and it may be that its efficiency, its life, depends upon the right action of some part which we can hardly discern. We know by our own experience that vigour and strength come in living things, from the harmonious combination of many small forces. So too it is in that greatest of all living bodies—the Church—which is the Body of Christ." [1]

And then—the question which often sorely tries us—as to results.

" Let me bid you not be anxious about results. Results are not for us. We know our work : God will give the issue as He sees good. We look back over the past history of the world, and we see that God waits ; and perhaps we can see, even with our feeble vision and poor judgment, that it was well He waited. Where He waits we can wait too. As we wait, if it be so, in the fulfilment of our work, we shall recognise that we have all an appointed office prepared for us by God. We shall offer the fulfilment of that office to Him in his Body the Church ; offer it in His strength, and for His glory ; that is, that we may make Him a little better known. So working and so waiting, we shall gain from day to day and from year to year, strength for

[1] *Incarnation and Common Life*, p. 410.

ourselves ; and, God helping us, we shall make
our Christian faith a little better known to those
without ; and we shall also make the splendid
inheritance which we have received in our own
loved Church a little better known to those who
at present often misunderstand it." [1]

Education

Here, as on the subject of Labour, it is only
possible to select a few passages illustrating the
lines of Bishop Westcott's teaching. Addresses on
the subject will be found in all his later volumes of
collected writings.

"Education is a spiritual relationship. It becomes operative through sympathy. The personal element in it is supreme. Faith and love
and religion can only be taught by those who
possess them. The teacher indeed communicates
himself, and then perhaps most effectively when
he is off his guard.

"We shall be agreed, I assume, that the object
of Education is to train for life, and for a special
occupation ; to train the whole man for all life,
for life seen and unseen, for the unseen through
the seen and in the seen ; to train citizens for
the Kingdom of God. As we believe in God
and the world to come, these must be master
thoughts. . . .

"We shall be agreed, once more, that the
noblest fruit of Education is character, and not

[1] *Incarnation and Common Life*, p. 418.

acquirements : character which makes the simplest life rich and beneficent, character which for a Christian is determined by a true vision of God, of whom, through whom, unto whom, are all things. This being agreed, we can form a just idea of the proper work of a teacher.

" At the same time he will strive that their knowledge shall be a growth and not a vestment, increasing from within and not added from without. He will make memory the handmaid of the mind and not its substitute : he will strive that all lessons shall, as far as possible, be of life and not of books, feeling that ' knowledge must be incorporated before it is real,' and that all that lives is of the living. In this way he will guard against the evil which the Egyptian king foresaw was likely to arise from the art of writing, that by this men ' would learn many things by hearsay without real knowledge, while, for the most part they would be utterly ignorant and unfit for social intercourse, having become seeming wise and not truly wise.' . . .

" The right use of leisure is an object of Education, not second—this is, you remember, the judgment of Aristotle—even to the right fulfilment of work. . . .

" Education is, so far as it is true, of the whole life, by the whole life." [1]

---

[1] All the above are from the two addresses in *Christian Aspects*.

Women's Work

" There is a message even for the present age in the fact emphatically recorded by St. John, that a woman was divinely charged to be the first herald of the Resurrection, the herald of the new life.

". . . Let mothers of every class feel that there are sicknesses of the soul which require the ministries of wise and tender affection, spiritual perils which need to be guarded against by watchful forethought, desires of the heart which crave the fulness of more than human love, and we shall be brought near to the consummation of our daily prayer in the advent of the Kingdom of God." [1]

" We have not yet sufficiently studied the part of women, or claimed their help. They have a power of spiritual vision which men have not. It was not an accident that a woman was the herald of the Resurrection. She may be yet again, in a fuller spiritual sense. To women great ideals are natural. They have an intuition of the whole of things. They have capacities for training and educating, which we have not yet used." [2]

General Counsels.

Under this head I have tried to gather together some of the most striking among those flashes of

[1] *Incarnation and Common Life*, p. 168 *et seq.*
[2] *Christian Aspects*, p. 199.

insight that meet us throughout Bishop Westcott's works—conveyed, very often, in a single sentence. They touch, as will be seen, on many subjects.   The two first are taken from his letters to personal friends.

On his fifty-fifth birthday, he wrote :

"Much, very much, seems less definite than once it did : less definite, but not, I trust, less real.   Every year makes me tremble more at the daring with which people speak of spiritual things.

"We must have faith.   It is just that that we are always wanting.   We wish to carry out our own plans.   For your work I have no fear.   You give all your past, yourself, to it ; and giving is the secret of true success. . . . There are many deaths and risings again. Is it not written over all, 'from strength to strength'?"

The following are from *The Incarnation and Common Life* :

"Offer yourselves to the fulfilment of the least duties without misgiving, but accept no rest which leaves you without service.   Be concentrated in the energy of personal action.   Be diffusive in the unity of special sympathy."

"We seem to exhaust ourselves in seeking material relief for special maladies."

"Whatever therefore may be your office, regard it as a fragment in an immeasurable ministry of love."

" Enthusiasm is reverence in action."

" We all of us require to learn, each in the fulfilment of his least office, that we have no rights, but duties, and no solitary joy."

" Violence can destroy, but it cannot construct. Love destroys the evil when it replaces the evil by the good."

The following are from *Lessons from Work* :

" To call out effort is as great a service to men as to satisfy a want."

" Our Faith is not seen, as it ought to be seen, to control our methods of business and of study ; our aims, and our relations to our fellow-men."

" A youth without visions means an old age without hope."

" Unattainable ideals are the guiding stars of life. They convert movement into progress. If we acknowledge them, they fix our goal, and enable us to strain towards it with undistracted and unwasted effort."

" Nothing is truly our own till we have communicated it to others."

" It is as perilous to live on borrowed opinions as on borrowed money ; the practice must end in intellectual or even in moral bankruptcy. Our Creed must be a spiritual growth and not a dress."

It is tempting to go on indefinitely with the work of selection, but it is best to stop. Enough has been given to show the treasures of thought on subjects of all kinds to be found in Bishop Westcott's writings, and those who desire more will do well to seek them for themselves. *The Incarnation and Common Life* offers perhaps the richest store of thoughts on social subjects ; and next after that, *Christian Aspects*, and *Lessons from Work* ; these being the three volumes that contain the largest number of the Bishop's addresses on the problems of the day. For the more directly personal and spiritual counsels, reference must be made, as will have been seen, to *all* his writings, for these thoughts pervade them all. And such thoughts are not for one, but for all. In proportion as we dwell upon them, we shall find that "the horizon of our vision will be widened as the years go on. We shall bring into more effective use from day to day the powers of the heavenly order. We shall find every burden fall off at last in the sight of the Cross and the Sepulchre. *In our patience we shall win our souls.*" [1]

[1] *Steps in the Christian Life*, p. 51.

X

THE STUDY OF
BISHOP WESTCOTT'S WRITINGS

THE STUDY OF BISHOP WESTCOTT'S WRITINGS

" Brethren, I have ventured to touch on great thoughts : thoughts strange, perhaps, and in part obscure, but yet thoughts which concern us most nearly in our daily life."—*Incarnation and Common Life.*

" Brethren, the thoughts on which we have touched open unfathomable depths of duty. But it is good for us to reflect on the greatness of God, which is as immeasurable as His love. And may He in His great mercy cleanse our dull eyes, and check our hasty tongues, and calm our impetuous reasonings ; and so, in the solemn calm, the vision of Him—Father, Son, and Holy Ghost—will take shape slowly before us."—*Christus Consummator.*

WIDESPREAD as is Bishop Westcott's influence, it will, I am convinced, be still more far-reaching when the most important aspect of his writings—their *practical* value—is more generally recognised. At present, the very greatness of his reputation as a scholar deters some readers, with the idea that his books are for scholars only. This is the very reason why I, who have no claim to scholarship, have presumed to write about them ; because the rich stores of help and guidance I have found there —" limited only by my own infirmities "—are within reach of every reader.

How can they best be gained ?

Not merely by reading this or any other volume

of selected passages. The best that these can do is to point to some of the many treasures to be had for the seeking. But that seeking, to be really fruitful, must be carried on by each one for himself.

For the help which Bishop Westcott's writings have for us lies not so much in individual thoughts or counsels—valuable as are many of these—as in the atmosphere into which he leads us ; an atmosphere of real, living, and most intensely personal trust in God, in which all life is viewed by the light not of its passing shows and passions, but of the things eternal and unseen. Such an atmosphere is strange to many of us ; to some it is simply devoid of meaning ; and to enter into it demands effort— often a long and painful one.

For this reason it is that Bishop Westcott's books are so commonly described as "difficult." Difficult undoubtedly they are, as life itself is diffi- cult, and as the Bishop recognised to the full. The words which follow, taken from one of his addresses, might have been spoken of all his teaching.

"In the endeavour to convey these thoughts, I have made, I know, a heavy demand upon the attention of those who have listened to me. The preacher can only speak from his heart and as he sees the truth. But such thoughts "—here comes the point above all others to be recog- nised—"are not so much difficult as strange. They are not mere speculations of the closet. They are not for scholars and students only, but for every believer who looks directly to Christ. They reach to the inmost depths of our

common life. . . . There is in the soul that
which leaps up in quick response to the greatest
hope. The soul was made to strive with unwearied desire towards an unattainable ideal.
Only let the principle of the Christian life,
which we too readily dwarf to the proportions
of conventional littleness, be recognised in its
breadth and power, and the life will clothe
itself in the form through which it will conquer." [1]

And yet again, elsewhere :

"Brethren, we have touched upon great
mysteries—mysteries to be kept and 'pondered
in our hearts.' In dealing with them, words
and thoughts are alike inadequate. So far as
these become definite, they tend to limit that
which is infinite. But their imperfection is not
unavailing if it encourages us to strive by the
help of the Holy Spirit—and it is a hard task—
to know that the revelation of God given to us
in the Incarnation is given by a living fact, not
in a speculation or a dogma. . . ." [2]

It is a great step towards gaining help from any
teacher, to understand clearly what help he has to
offer. And so, in setting to work to study Bishop
Westcott's writings, it is worth while to keep in
view the three truths that were constantly before
his mind.

First—That no human teacher can make clear
divine mysteries. Only God Himself can do this,

[1] *Victory of the Cross*, p. 106.
[2] *Christus Consummator*, p. 158.

by the working of His Holy Spirit, and the utmost that earthly help can achieve is to lead us to learn of Him. As Bishop Westcott has said of Bible study :

> "No one can make another understand what the Bible is : the assurance must come from the Spirit of God, speaking to the individual soul."[1]

Next—That the deepest of mysteries have the most practical value in daily life.

> "The noblest truths are not given us for an intellectual luxury, still less for a moral opiate or a spiritual charm. They are for the inspiration of our whole being, for the hallowing and for the bracing of every power, outward and inward, with which we are endowed, for use in the busy fields of common duty. . . . And so the greatest of all truths—the truth of the Incarnation—reaches to the innermost recesses of the single life, that it may rouse and guide and sustain him who has welcomed it."[2]

Last—but by no means least—that this personal value of great truths cannot be made our own without continued effort.

> "Can we suppose that the highest knowledge, and the highest knowledge alone, is to be gained without effort, without preparation, without discipline, by a simple act of memory? Must the eye and the hand of the artist be trained

---

[1] *Lessons from Work.*
[2] *Christus Consummator*, p. 148.

through long years to discern and to portray subtle harmonies of form and colour, while that spiritual faculty by which we enter on the unseen may be safely left unexercised until some sudden emergency calls it into play." [1]

Truths, these are, that sorely need to be insisted on at the present time ; not for the sake of Bishop Westcott's writings only, but for the whole question of the Christian Faith. Why is it that so many professing Christians suffer themselves to be led astray by one or another of the many forms of old heresies in new guise ? Why is it, above all, that they profess so eagerly to have found in these what the old-fashioned Faith of the Church has failed to give them ? Why, but because they have studied their new Creeds with the pains they refused to spend upon the old. The disciples of " Christian Science," for example, do not shrink from the daily " exercises " demanded of them, nor from the hours of study needed to enter into the teaching of the strange volume in which they are bidden to find their Gospel. Misleading as that teaching is— utterly false in many of its aspects—yet it does lead the thoughts of its followers to the power of things unseen, and so undoubtedly does give them that which they have never given themselves time to find in the Gospel taught and treasured by the Church of Christ, " which is His Body."

Here, surely, is the special value of Bishop Westcott's teaching in these days of false spirituality, and restless efforts to find some new and speedier

[1] *Christus Consummator*, p. 85.

way of mastering the powers that lie beyond sight and sense. For it is just those very powers that he sets forth as the essential heart and centre of the Christian Faith. He has left us in his life a striking instance of these powers applied to daily work and problems; and in his writings he has shown us how such results may be achieved in the way that He who is the Way laid down for us, and that His Church has followed ever since.

Perhaps the phrase that recurs most frequently throughout the Bishop's writings is that in which he loves to insist, again and again, that the Faith of Christ, the Revelation of God, the working of the Holy Spirit, "*is not a vain thing for us, for it is our life.*"

That one sentence may be said to give the sum of his teaching. It is the same thought that runs through all he wrote, only differently applied and expressed. For readers, therefore, unacquainted with his books, the best advice is to begin with whichever of these seem the easiest and the most interesting. In this way they will become familiar both with the thoughts themselves, and with the mode of expression, and so can follow them into their more difficult forms.

Take, for example, the two books dealing specially with the Resurrection—the *Gospel of the Resurrection* and the *Revelation of the Risen Lord.* The former of these contains the Bishop's deepest teaching on the subject; "the only one of my books that I care much about," as he himself wrote of it; the spring of far-reaching thoughts and glorious hope to those who have mastered it. But to do so is at first not

easy, and demands an effort which well may daunt
the unaccustomed reader; whereas the *Revelation*,
written in short chapters of picturesque and vivid
beauty, appeals to every one. The same thoughts
are there, only not worked out so fully, and this first
glimpse of them in a simpler form, makes it far easier
to follow them out in the more difficult companion
volume.

Any book of Bishop Westcott's that we fail to
master is best put aside for awhile, and exchanged
for one that appeals to us more directly. We shall
come back to the more difficult one some day, when
things unseen have grown more real to us, and shall
find in its pages the very message that we need.
Words which once seemed devoid of meaning will
speak straight to the heart; and the thoughts which
once were far beyond our reach, and therefore dim
and dark, grow clear and glorious when the soul, in
Browning's phrase, "has grown to match."

This happens again and again to the earnest
student of Bishop Westcott's writings. Those which
were at first passed over as " obscure " are seen to be
only " indistinct from excess of light." For the
reason why his thoughts are hard to follow is not
that he saw truth less clearly than most people, but
that he saw more of its splendour. The glory must
needs be dazzling, yet in its light life gains a fuller
meaning. And to show the force of this meaning in
the varying circumstances of life is Bishop Westcott's
special work.

The *Revelation of the Father* is another of the
Bishop's simpler works, at any rate in form of expression, for the thoughts go very deep. So they do

also in *Christus Consummator*, which nevertheless is one of the most intensely attractive of all his books. *Steps in the Christian Life* is almost the shortest and simplest of them all, and is written with a direct and personal appeal very helpful to those in need of practical guidance. Any readers beginning their study of his writings with one of these, or with the historical sketches in *Social Aspects*, would assuredly be led on to seek further. The later volumes of collected addresses on various subjects form also, of course, a valuable introduction to Bishop Westcott's teaching.

For Notes on the Bishop's *Commentaries*, see the chapter kindly added here by the Rev. Arthur Westcott. These Notes, as well as all the rest of this book, have been written with the single purpose of bringing an ever-widening circle of readers into touch with " one who has laboured unceasingly to bring his countrymen face to face with the New Testament Scriptures ; one for whom Christian truth is the realm of light from which alone the dwellers on earth receive whatever power they have to read the riddle of the world or choose their steps aright ; one to whom the Christian Society is almost as a watch-word, and who hears in every social distress of the time a cry for help which only a social interpretation of the Gospel can give." [1]

[1] From Dr. Hort's sermon, preached at Bishop Westcott's consecration.

BISHOP WESTCOTT'S
COMMENTARIES

By the Rev. ARTHUR WESTCOTT

BISHOP WESTCOTT'S COMMENTARIES

THE late Dr Thompson, Master of Trinity, speaking in 1851 of Mr. Westcott, whom he had examined on more than one occasion, said—"In all respects he approved himself a scholar, as compared with scholars, of more than the usual accomplishments, and much more than usual promise."

This talent of scholarship Mr. Westcott determined from the first to use and improve in the service of Christ. So it came to pass that at the age of twenty-five he was enabled to produce a theological work which still survives,[1] and was, all things considered, "an extraordinary *tour de force.*" It showed that the author had, in his investigations, covered the whole field of theological learning from the early Christian fathers "to the latest German critic," and "brought to the discussion thoughts of almost Apostolic depth and insight." From the very first there were some critics who recognised in the young theologian "a learning and accuracy which commanded respect and confidence," combined with "the no less valuable faculties of lucid arrangement and graceful and facile expression."

Other works which followed the first effort served to increase the scholar's reputation for learning,

[1] *An Introduction to the Study of the Gospels.*

accuracy, and fair-mindedness. When, therefore, Dr. Westcott undertook the very heavy responsibility of producing a Commentary on the Gospel of St. John, not the least of his qualifications was that he had already laboured successfully in Biblical study. Another of his qualifications was that he was a really good Greek scholar, " which is not a matter of course, even in highly popular and distinguished commentators." But, above all, he was a profoundly spiritual man, and thus fitted to enter into the deep truths contained in the Gospel. He has himself remarked that Augustine, who used an imperfect Latin translation, was a more successful expositor of St. John than Chrysostom, who was an accomplished Greek scholar. Accurate scholarship, profound thought, thorough work, and a reverent tone, are all required in the interpreter of Holy Writ ; but, with all these present, there may yet be the one thing lacking— spiritual insight. Hereby, as an expositor, Augustine excelled Chrysostom. By such a faculty,—by what one has described as " the intense brooding nature of his intelligence,"—Dr. Westcott was eminently qualified to interpret St. John to our age.

The Gospel of St. John has been the very centre of the sceptical attack, and on this account the introduction to the Gospel is of primary importance. The introduction in Dr. Westcott's *Commentary* fills ninety-seven pages of closely printed matter, and had it not been for the writer's marked gift of condensed expression, it might have covered many more pages. Masses of literature have been studied, and the positions of various writers carefully considered ; but this fact is not always obvious, because the writer does not call attention to it. He has been accused of taking "a good deal for granted," because he has not devoted a disproportionate amount of space to detailed criticism of the views of others. He has, however, furnished the materials for their refutation, and trusted his readers so to use them. For example, the treatment of Justin Martyr's testimony to the Gospel, which seems " perfunctory " to one, strikes another as being a model "not less of conciseness than of candour." But in the consideration of the Johannine authorship of the Fourth Gospel, Dr. Westcott's argument from the internal evidence is the most original feature of his work. By a chain of argument, which to many seems absolutely conclusive, he proves from the Gospel itself that the author was a Jew—a Jew of Palestine, an eyewitness, an Apostle, and finally St. John, the son of Zebedee.

Amongst the most interesting sections of the introduction are those which deal with the historical exactness of the Gospel, and with the Evangelist's vivid portraiture of character. If we are tempted to regard the Fourth Gospel as a work of fiction because we cannot recognise the Christ of the Synoptists in the Christ of St. John, or the facts of the Synoptic Record in the facts of St. John's Gospel, a passage such as the following will hearten us :

" Does the author of the Fourth Gospel forfeit his claim to observe accuracy of fact because the facts are selected with a view to a definite purpose ? He professes to write, as we have seen, in the hope of creating in others the faith which he holds himself.   Now, that faith is in reality a special interpretation of a history drawn from a special interpretation of One Life.   We may, therefore, modify our question, and ask, Does the Evangelist forfeit his claim to be a truthful historian because he turns his eye steadily to the signs of the central laws of being?   The answer to the question must be sought finally in the conditions of the historian's work.   These conditions include in every case choice, compression, combination of materials, and he fulfils his work rightly who chooses, compresses, and combines his materials according to a certain vital proportion.   In other words, the historian, like the poet, cannot but interpret the facts which he records. The truth of history is simply the truth of the interpretation of an infinitude of details contemplated together.   The simplest statement of a result presents a broad generalisation of particulars.   The generalisation may be true or false ; it may be ruled by an outward or by an inward principle, but in any case it only represents a total impression of the particulars seen in one way.   It does not represent either all the particulars or all the impressions which they are capable of producing.   What is called pure ' objective ' history is a pure phantom.   No one could specify, and no one would be willing to specify, all the separate details which man's most imperfect observation can distinguish as elements in any one ' fact,' and the least reflection shows that there are other elements not less numerous or less important than those open to our observation which cannot be observed by us, and which yet go to the fulness of the 'fact.' The subjectivity of history is consequently a mere question of degree. A writer who looks at the outside of things, and reproduces the impression which this would convey to average men, is as far from the whole truth as the writer who brings his whole power to bear upon an individual realisation of it. Thus every record of a fact is necessarily limited to the record of representative details concerning it. The truthfulness of the historian as a narrator lies, therefore, in his power of selecting those details so as to convey to others the true idea of the fact which he has himself formed. In this respect the literary accuracy of any number of details is no guarantee for the accuracy of the impression conveyed by the sense of them regarded as a whole ; and it is no paradox to say that a 'true' detail which disturbs the proportion of the picture becomes in the connection false."

From the section on " The Characters " the following fragment is derived :

" The contrast beetween Nicodemus and the woman of Samaria, the two to whom Christ, according to the narrative of John, first unfolds the mysteries of the kingdom, cannot fail to be noticed. A Rabbi stands side by side with a woman who is not even qualified, in popular opinion, to be a scholar ; a Jew with a Samaritan ; a dignified member of the Council with a fickle, impulsive villager. The circumstances of the

discourses are not less different. The one is
held in Jerusalem, the other almost under the
shadow of the schismatical temple in Gerizim ;
the one in the house by night, the other in the
daylight by the well-side. Christ is sought in
the one case, in the other He asks first, that so
He may give afterwards. The discourses themselves open out distinct views of the kingdom.
To Nicodemus Christ speaks of a new birth, of
spiritual influence witnessed by spiritual life, of
the elevation of the Son of Man, in whom earth
and Heaven were united. To the Samaritan He
speaks of the water of life, which should satisfy
a thirst assumed to be real, of a worship in spirit
and truth, of Himself as the Christ who should
teach all things."

It had been Dr. Westcott's original purpose to
join his *Commentary on St. John* to the Greek text
of the Gospel, and he had prepared much matter
not available for use in his published work ; but he
was well content to present the labour of many
years in a form accessible to ordinary English
readers, and to relegate some matters of less interest
to general readers to Additional Notes. The notes
are models of brevity, being unencumbered with
interpretations which the writer believed to be false,
and so phrased as to convey more than they actually
express of the meaning grasped. There is never a
superfluous word, but thoughts fresh and suggestive
are compressed into the smallest compass consistent
with intelligibility. The following is a specimen of
the writer's expository method and power :

" ' *They shall become one flock, one Shepherd* '—
they shall become — they shall present the
accomplishment of the ancient prophecy (Ezek.
xxxiv. 23). That which ' is ' in the eternal
counsel and truth of things ' becomes ' in human
history, and this stage by stage and not by one
complete transformation. . . . The translation of
' fold ' for ' flock ' has been most disastrous in
idea and in influence. The change in the
original from fold to flock is most striking, and
reveals a new thought as to the future relations
of Jew and Gentile. Elsewhere stress is laid
upon their corporate union (Rom. xi. 17) and
upon the admission of the Gentiles to the Holy
City (Isa. ii. 3), but here the bond of fellowship
is shown to lie in the common relation to one
Lord. . . . It may be added that the oblitera-
tion of this essential distinction between the fold
and the flock in many of the later Western
versions of this passage indicates, as it appears, a
tendency of Roman Christianity, and has served
in no small degree to confirm and extend the
false claims of the Roman See. . . . It would
perhaps be impossible for any correction now
to do away with the effects which a translation undeniably false has produced on popular
ecclesiastical ideas."

To mention just one other note: that on John i. 18,
is interesting, because it was asserted that the N.T.
Revisers shrank from accepting the best-attested
reading in this passage lest they should inflict too
severe a blow on popular or orthodox theology.

Dr. Westcott, however, adopts the reading *God only begotten*, and expounds it so as to confirm rather than weaken orthodox doctrine. He says:

> "'One who is God only begotten' or 'God the only Son,' One of whom it can be predicated that He is unique in His Being and God, is none other than 'the only begotten Son.' The word Son—the only begotten Son—carries with it identity of essence. The article in the one case defines as completely as the predicate in the other. But the best-attested reading has the advantage of combining the two great predicates of the Word which have been previously indicated—*i.e.* His Deity and His Sonship."

The question of the reading is discussed in an Additional Note. Other Additional Notes which have attracted attention are those on "The World," "The Son of Man," "The Brazen Serpent," "The Unnamed Feast," "The Comforter," "My Father is Greater than I," "St. Peter's Denial."

Dr. Westcott's *Commentary on the Epistles of St. John*, which was published some years after that on the Gospel, had the advantage of being issued with the Greek text. Thus the writer was enabled to expound more carefully the slightest turns of language and, so far as he was able, exhaust their meaning. Of course there were critics who regarded this careful attention to the exact language of the Apostle as "artificial trifling," and charged the expositor with "drawing from his own spiritual consciousness and putting the product into the Johannine epistles."[1]

[1] *The Academy.*

Such criticisms, linked as they are in friendly companionship with the expressed opinion that the repetitions found in the Epistle are " signs of the feebleness of age," [1] are interesting to students of Dr. Westcott's writings merely as showing to what a pass we may come if we are not to attach any special importance to the writer's exact phraseology. It will be obvious that those who can hold such views are in a different intellectual and spiritual hemisphere from Dr. Westcott's. In explanation of his general method of exegesis, Dr. Westcott says :

> " It formed no part of my design to collect and discuss the conflicting opinions which have been held on the structure of the writings or on the interpretation of separate passages. Such a labour is indeed of the deepest interest and utility ; but it appeared to me that I might help the student more by giving the results at which I had arrived, and by indicating the lines of inquiry by which they have been reached. In pursuing this end it has been my main desire to call attention to the minutest points of language, construction, order, as serving to illustrate the meaning of St. John. I do not venture to pronounce that any variation is trivial or unimportant. The exact words are for us the decisive expression of the Apostle's thoughts. . . . I do not venture to set aside the letter of a document till it has been found to be untenable."

[1] *The Academy.*

So anxious was Dr. Westcott not to cumber his notes with the conflicting opinions of writers of all ages that he has barely admitted mention of any commentator of a later age than Bede or Thomas Aquinas. But, although it is not immediately apparent, he has carefully studied writers ancient and modern, and we can rest assured that little, if any, of what they have said has been unconsidered by him. In the place of a congeries of contradictory opinions, tending to confuse and mislead the student, he presents us with a definite interpretation uttered with a quiet confidence begotten of laborious research and prayerful thought.

As samples of the notes contained in the work, we may cite those on 1 John ii. 5 (the love of God), and 1 John ii. 12, both of which I quote in full :

"ἡ ἀγάπη τοῦ θεοῦ] *caritas Dei* V., *dilectio Dei* Aug., *the love of God.* The phrase, which occurs in the Epistle first here and henceforth throughout it, is ambiguous and may mean, according as the gen. is taken *subj.* or *obj.*, either (1) the love which God shows, or (2) the love of which God is the object. It may also mean more generally (3) the love which is characteristic of God whether it is regarded as shown by God or by man through His help. Generally the genitive after ἀγάπη in the N.T. is *subj.*, and defines those who feel or show love : 1 Thess. iii. 6 ; 2 Thess. i. 3 ; Phil. i. 9 ; Col. i. 8 ; Philem. 5, 7 ; Apoc. ii. 4, 19. Once it marks the object of love : 2 Thess. ii. 10, ἡ ἀγ. τῆς ἀληθείας. But the object is more commonly ex-

pressed by εἰς: 1 Thess. iii. 12 ; Col. i. 4 ;
1 Pet. iv. 8. Comp. Ign. *Mart.* 1 ; [Clem. R.]
fragm. 1 (Jacobson).

"In St. Paul 'the love of God,' with the
doubtful exception of 2 Thess. iii. 5, always
means the love which is shown by God, which
comes from God : 2 Cor. xiii. 13 ; Rom. v. 5 ;
viii. 39 ; Eph. ii. 4 ; and so also 'the love of
Christ' is the love which Christ has shown and
shows : 2 Cor. v. 14 ; Rom. viii. 35 ; Eph. iii. 19.
Comp. Ign. *ad Trall.* 6 ; *ad Rom.* inscr. In like
manner 'the love of the Spirit' (Rom. xv. 30)
is that love which the Spirit kindles and sustains.
The phrase 'the love of God' does not occur
in the LXX.

" The usage of St. John is less simple than that
of St. Paul. In 1 John iv. 9 '*the love of God*'
is evidently the love which God has shown
(comp. c. v. 9, ἡ μαρτυρία τοῦ θεοῦ), and this
love is declared to be the spring of all love.
'*His love*' (*v.* 12) becomes effective in man.
This conception of the love of God as communicated by God to man is plainly expressed
in 1 John iii. 1, *the Father hath given to us love*
(comp. c. iv. 7, 16). Love such as God Himself
feels — 'divine love' — becomes therefore an
endowment of the Christian. In this sense 'the
love of God' in the believer calls for deeds of
love to the brethren (c. iii. 17). At the same
time God is Himself the object of the love of
which He is the source and the rule : c. v. 3
(comp. John xiv. 15, 31) ; ii. 15 (ἡ ἀγ. τοῦ
πατρός).

"It appears therefore most probable that the fundamental idea of 'the love of God' in St. John is 'the love which God has made known, and which answers to His nature.' This love communicated to man is effective in him towards the brethren and towards God Himself. But however it may be manifested, the essential conception that it is a love divine in its origin and character is not lost. Comp. John xv. 9 f.

"According to this interpretation the phrase corresponds with the 'righteousness of God' (Rom. i. 17, etc.), the 'peace of God' (Phil. iv. 7).

"The phrase occurs twice only in the Gospels: Luke xi. 42; John v. 42. In each case the rendering 'love to God' is admissible, but this rendering does not seem to exhaust the meaning (comp. Clem. R. 1 Cor. 49).

"In the present passage there can be little doubt that c. iv. 9 defines the meaning. 'The love of God' is God's love towards man welcomed and appropriated by man. The thought of action is throughout connected with the thought of what God has done. The Christian 'knows the love of God,' and it becomes in him a spring of love, attaining its complete development in human life through vital obedience.

The second note quoted is that on a passage which is well known to Bible scholars as a famous *crux interpretum.* It runs:

"πείσομεν . . . ὅτι ἐὰν καταγινώσκῃ . . . ὅτι μείζων . . . πάντα] *suademus (suadeamus, suade-bimus) quoniam si reprehenderit nos (male senserit*

Aug.) *cor nostrum major est Deus corde nostro et novit omnia* V. (*we*) *shall assure our heart before Him whereinsoever our heart condemn us, because God is greater than our heart and knoweth all things*. The many conflicting interpretations of this passage spring out of the different transla- tions of (1) the verb πείσομεν, and (2) the double conjunction or relative ὅτι (ὅ τι).

" 1. Thus if we take the sense *persuade* for the verb, there are two groups of renderings pos- sible : the first (*a*), in which the clauses which follow give the substance of that of which we are satisfied ; and the second (β), in which this substance is supposed to be supplied by the reader.

"(*a*) In the first case there are two possible views :

"(*a*) The second ὅτι may be simply resump- tive : *We shall persuade our heart, that, if our heart condemn us, that,* I say, *God is greater. . . .*

"(*b*) Or the first ὅτι may be taken as the relative : *We shall persuade our heart, where- insoever our heart condemn us, that God is greater. . . .*

" Against both these interpretations it may be urged, as it seems, with decisive force, that the conclusion is not one which flows naturally from the premiss. The consciousness of a sincere love of the brethren does not furnish the basis of the conviction of the sovereign greatness of God.

"(β) If the substance of that of which we shall be persuaded is mentally supplied, as, 'that we are of the truth,' or 'that our prayers are heard,' there are again two possible interpretations :

"(a) The second ὅτι may be taken as resumptive in the sense *because*: *we shall persuade our heart, because if our heart condemn us, because*, I say, *God is greater.* . . .

"(b) Or again the first ὅτι may be taken as the relative: *we shall persuade our heart whereinsoever our heart condemn us, because God is greater.* . . .

"It appears to be a fatal objection to both these views that just *that* has to be supplied which the sense given to the verb leads the reader to expect to be clearly expressed. And further, it may be remarked that while the use of a resumptive ὅτι is quite intelligible after the introduction of a considerable clause, it is very unnatural after the insertion of a few words.

"2. If on the other hand the verb be taken in the sense 'we shall assure,' 'we shall still and tranquillise the fears and misgivings of our heart,' there are yet two modes of completing the sentence :

"(a) The second ὅτι may be taken as resumptive in the sense of *because*: *we shall assure our hearts, because if our heart condemn us, because*, I say, *God is greater.* Such a resumptive use of the particle has, however, been shown to be very harsh.

"(β) There remains then the adoption of the first ὅτι as the relative: *We shall assure our heart, whereinsoever our heart condemn us, because God is greater.* . . .

"This sense falls in completely with the context, and flows naturally from the Greek.

"But an ambiguity still remains. In what sense is the superior greatness of God to be understood? Is it the ground of our exceeding need? or of our sure confidence? Both interpretations can be drawn from the words. (1) We shall then, and then only, still our heart, in whatsoever it may condemn us, because we know that the judgment of God must be severer than our own judgment, and so apart. from fellowship with Him we can have no hope. Or (2) We shall then still our heart in whatsoever it may condemn us, because we are in fellowship with God, and that fact assures us of His sovereign mercy. The latter sense seems to be required by the whole context. See below."

Of the Additional Notes, those on 1 John iv. 12 (the use of θεός and ὁ θεός), and 3 Ep. 7 (the Divine Name) have been specially noticed.

The volume is enriched with three interesting essays which occupy one hundred and twenty-three pages. The first of these, entitled "The Two Empires: the Church and the World," illustrates the hindrance to Christian progress involved in the worship of the Roman Emperor. The second is entitled "The Gospel of Creation," and, though it deals with a subject which is usually regarded as being of purely speculative fascination, has been found by many to be both interesting and instructive. The subject of the essay is the old theme of mediæval scholasticism, namely, Whether, if man had not sinned, the Lord Christ would have taken upon him our flesh. Herein Dr. Westcott is "frankly Scotist," and holds to the belief that the Incarnation was part of the divine purpose in Creation. But he will not allow that the subject is but a curious fancy of a past age. For he had found "light in face of great problems which seem likely to grow more urgent every day" from the view which he maintained. That view he held to be illuminating, because:

> "It presents to us the highest manifestation of divine love as answering to the idea of man, and not as dependent upon that which lay outside the Father's Will.
>
> "It reveals to us how the divine purpose is fulfilled in unexpected and unimaginable ways in spite of man's selfishness and sin.
>
> "It indicates, at least, how that unity to which many physical and historical researches point is not only to be found in a dispersive connection of multitudinous parts, but is summed up finally in one life.
>
> "It helps us to feel a little more, and this is the sum of all, what the Incarnation is, what it involves, what it promises, what it enforces, what it inspires; that Fact which we strive to believe, and which is ever escaping from us; that Fact which sets before us with invincible majesty Christ's 'power to subdue all things to Himself.'"

The third essay is entitled "The Relation of

Christianity to Art," and presents a historical study of the contrast between the original attitude of Christendom to Art and its subsequent adoption of Art to the service of Christ. Dr. Westcott, it may be remarked, was much perplexed by the voices of several critics who could not perceive the connection of these essays with his subject. He was troubled that persons should conclude that he had merely seized an opportunity of drawing from his desk some miscellaneous writings which might set forth "the many-sidedness of his ingenious and fertile mind." For to him they seemed to be, as they were from the first intended to be, an integral part of his work.

The last published of Dr. Westcott's *Commentaries*, that *On the Epistle to the Hebrews*, is regarded by many as the greatest of his expository works. For many years before he produced it he had "been recognised as one of the most profound theologians, and one of the most thorough scholars of those who speak our mother-tongue." Others give expression to this same feeling in language more emphatic, which it is unnecessary to quote. A sober and sympathetic critic has borne the following weighty testimony :

"His is one of the best and finest types of English scholarship. Exact and accurate in his methods, a skilled grammarian, and of wide and extensive learning, he has also that tinge of mysticism, that sympathy with the ultimate mystery of things, without which a man tends to become commonplace."

The work on the Hebrews was very dear to the writer himself. It was the last that he was able to complete, before his elevation to the Episcopate compelled him to divert his energies into other channels. He says of it :

> " No work on which I have ever been allowed to spend many years of continuous labour has had for me the same intense human interest as the study of the Epistle to the Hebrews."

For a general description of the work I cannot do better than quote the following :[1] "The book attracts the student at once by its admirable method, and by a clearness of arrangement which is aided by good typography. As a writer, Dr. Westcott is master of a style which is as weighty as it is the reverse of ponderous. The contrast which he presents in many respects to some of the best-known German commentators is complete. With an acumen as remarkable and with a learning as minute and as extensive as theirs, he exhibits neither their interminable verbosity nor their egotistic straining after originality ; he is free from their empty theorising ; he never for a moment allows his ingenuity to run away with his sobriety of judgment ; he indulges in no idle rhetoric. We might challenge a critic to indicate any point of importance that he has missed. There are materials in several of his more important notes sufficient for as many separate treatises, each of considerable length. Yet the whole is so condensed and simplified that it is all compressed into a volume of five hundred pages. Nor is the spirit in which the book is written less admirable than its substance. Dr. Westcott, with the grave modesty of real learning, never dogmatises. He is not

[1] From *The Guardian*.

ashamed of confessing that a problem is insoluble.
Not that he is hazy in his judgments : on the contrary, he is always as definite in statement as he is
lucid in exposition. Need we add that a tone of
the deepest religious feeling pervades the book in
every line ? "

The introduction, which covers about sixty-five
pages, deals exhaustively with the many critical
questions that have gathered round the Epistle,
including those of the original language in which it
was written, and its authorship. Internal evidence
—the use of Greek words that have no Aramaic
equivalents, the use of the Septuagint, not merely in
quotation, but also as a basis for formal argument—
leads Dr. Westcott to decide clearly against the
theory of a Hebrew original. In the matter of
authorship we are, he says, left "with a negative
conclusion." After considering the arguments ad-
duced in favour of the various suggested authors,
he rises superior to "our natural unwillingness to
frankly confess our ignorance on a matter which
excites our interest," and concludes his investigation
with these words :

"And yet in this case the confession of ignorance is really the confirmation of an inspiriting
faith. We acknowledge the divine authority
of the Epistle, self-attested and ratified by
the illuminated consciousness of the Christian
Society ; we measure what would have been our
loss if it had not been included in our Bible ;
and we confess that the wealth of spiritual power
was so great in the early Church that he who

was empowered to commit to writing this view of the fulness of the Truth has not, by that conspicuous service, even left his name for the grateful reverence of later ages. ' It was enough that the faith and the love were there to minister to the Lord ' " (Matt. xxvi. 13).

The last section of the introduction, which treats of " The Epistle of the Hebrews and the Epistle of Barnabas," has been described as " a piece of work which exhibits all the best qualities of Canon Westcott as a thinker and expositor." It concludes with the following summary :

" In a word, in the Epistle of Barnabas there is no sense of the divine discipline of men, of an education of the world corresponding to the growth of humanity : no recognition of the importance of outward circumstances, of rules and observances, as factors in religious life : no acknowledgment of a relation of proportion between spiritual lessons and a people's capacity. It is an illustration of the same fundamental fault that we find in the Epistle not only a complete rejection of the letter of the Levitical system, but also an imperfect and inadequate view of Christian institutions. On the other hand we have, in Hebrews i. 1-4, a view of the unfolding and infolding of the divine counsel in creation of infinite fulness. The end is there seen to be the true consummation of the beginning. We discern that one message is conveyed by the different modes of God's communication to His people ; that one voice speaks through many envoys ; that at last the spoken word is gathered up and fulfilled in the present Son. We have not yet mastered all the teaching of the pregnant words ; yet even now we can perceive how the thoughts which they convey characterise the whole Epistle ; how they rose naturally out of the circumstances of the early Church ; and by comparison with the Epistle of Barnabas, how far they transcended the common judgment of the time. Under this aspect the Epistle to the Hebrews, by its composition and its history, throws light upon the ideas of Inspiration and a Canon of Scripture. On the one side we see how the Spirit of God uses special powers, tendencies, and conditions, things personal and things social, for the expression of a particular aspect of the Truth ; and on the other side we see how the enlightened consciousness of the Church was in due time led to recognise that teaching as authoritative which was at first least in harmony with prevailing forms of thought."

The detailed exegesis reveals the same grammatical accuracy, wide learning, and deep insight into ethical, spiritual, and historical truth which had characterised former work. It was still objected by some that the attention to minutiæ was overdone. Warned by previous experience, the writer anticipates this objection, and in the course of his remarks says :

" I should not, of course, maintain that the fulness of meaning which can be recognised in

the phrases of a book like the Epistle to the
Hebrews was consciously apprehended by the
author, though he seems to have used the
resources of literary art with more distinct
design than any other of the Apostles. But
clearness of spiritual vision brings with it a
corresponding precision and force of expression
through which the patient interpreter can attain
little by little to that which the prophet saw."

Two striking features of the *Commentary* itself are
"its extraordinary thoroughness," and its "constant
instructiveness." "More can be learnt from any two
or three of its pages than from a volume of average
theology." Such being the case, it becomes the
more difficult to call attention to any special notes ;
but, taking another for my guide, I will select por-
tions from notes which may "convey some slight
idea of the concentrated wisdom which characterises"
the mass. The first deals with the word ὑπόστασις,
which Dr. Westcott translates by Essence (i. 3).
After indicating the primary meaning of the word
as being "that which stands beneath" as a "sedi-
ment" or "foundation" or "ground of support,"
and the derived senses of "firmness," "confidence,"
"reality," that in virtue of which a thing is what it
is, "the essence of anything," the note continues :

"When this meaning of 'essence' was applied
to the Divine Being, two distinct usages arose in
the course of debate. If men looked at the
Holy Trinity under the aspect of the one Godhead, there was only one ὑπόστασις, one divine
essence. If, on the other hand, they looked at

each Person in the Holy Trinity, then that by
which each Person is what He is—His ὑπόστασις—was necessarily regarded as distinct, and
there were three ὑποστάσεις. In the first case
ὑπόστασις as applied to the One Godhead was
treated as equivalent to οὐσία : in the other case
it was treated as equivalent to πρόσωπον.

" As a general rule the Eastern (Alexandrine)
Fathers adopted the second mode of speech
affirming the existence of three ὑποστάσεις (real
Persons) in the Godhead ; while the Western
Fathers affirmed the unity of one ὑπόστασις
(essence) in the Holy Trinity. . . . Hence
many mediæval and modern writers have taken
ὑπόστασις in the sense of ' Person' here. But
this use of the word is much later than the
apostolic age ; and it is distinctly inappropriate
in this connection. The Son is not the image,
the expression of the ' Person' of God. On
the other hand, He is the expression of the
' essence' of God. He brings the Divine before
us at once perfectly and definitely according to
the measure of our powers."

For the second specimen we go no further than
the next verse, where there is a brief comment on
the Session of Christ " on the right hand " of God.
The note runs :

" The idea is of course of dignity and not of
place (Dextra Dei ubique est). All local asso-
ciation must be excluded. . . . We, as we at
present are, are forced to think in terms of
space ; but it does not follow that this limitation

belongs to the perfection of humanity. . . . This
Session of Christ at the right hand of God—the
figure is only used of the Incarnate Son—is
connected with His manifold activity as King
(Acts ii. 33, Eph. i. 21, Col. iii. 1, ch. x. 12) and
Priest (1 Pet. iii. 22, ch. viii. 1, ch. xii. 2) and
Intercessor (Rom. viii. 34).   Comp. Acts vii. 55."

In addition to the running commentary there are
a considerable number of Additional Notes, grammatical, critical, and doctrinal.   Included among these
are two very important notes on the prae-Christian
Priesthood, and the prae-Christian idea of Sacrifice.
Dr. Westcott's conclusions on the supremely important subject of the Priesthood have been summarised
as follows :

" The foundation of this is laid in the very instincts
of human nature.   Sacrifice is treated as the highest
expression of the life of man : ' it is the response of
love to love, of the son to the Father, the rendering
to God in grateful use of that which has been
received from Him.'   Hence it is independent of
sin, though sin adds to it the necessity of expiation
and atonement ; and this latter element was specially
emphasised in the Jewish religion.   The consciousness of sin hinders the direct approach to God ; man
looks for some one through whom this access shall
be gained.   This is the work of the priest ; his duty
is to establish the connection of man with God, and
secondarily of man with man.   The idea of the
priesthood is thus universal ; and the chief forms
which it has taken both in the nations and in the
Jewish people are enumerated.   It is then shown

how Christ takes up the various conceptions of priesthood. He was the representative of the Aaronic priesthood in His earthly lifetime, offering Himself to God, and by His blood reopening access to the Father, and fulfilling all that was implied in the Day of Atonement. Further, He is now in His ascended life the representative of the Royal High Priesthood of Melchizedek, where He pleads for man by His presence before the Father's throne, and brings the prayers and praises of His people to God. He has won for man redemption, forgiveness, atonement, reconciliation :

" ' By His perfect fulfilment of the destiny of man under the conditions of the fall, He has brought within man's reach the end of his creation.' " [1]

The volume concludes with an essay "On the Use of the Old Testament in the Epistle." Dr. Westcott examines the range of the quotations—that is, from what books they are taken—then how they are cited, and their text, and then proceeds to inquire into the principles on which they are interpreted by the author of the Epistle. " The spirit in which students should approach the perplexing questions of Old Testament criticism could not be better described than it is in this last essay."

The last of Dr. Westcott's *Commentaries*—that on the Epistle to the Ephesians—has not yet been published. To this work he devoted, during the years of his episcopate, all the slight leisure time afforded by his annual holidays. At such times he was always full of it, and he noted with thankfulness in his Daily Text-Book its practical completion. For

[1] Quoted from Dr. Westcott.

the past two years the book has hovered on the verge of publication, and it is devoutly to be wished that the long-deferred hope of studying it may soon be realised.

I cannot conclude these brief notes without giving utterance to one word about the famous Westcott and Hort Greek Testament; that work, undertaken in collaboration with his old friend Dr. Hort, being the greatest monument of Dr. Westcott's learning and industry. One point that struck me in a rapid perusal of masses of correspondence on this subject, was the anxious care devoted by the editors to the divisions of the text when that had been finally settled. This is of course but a small part of the whole, and is not a matter of textual criticism at all, but I cannot refrain from remarking that a survey of the correspondence carried on by two such men in discussing, *e.g.*, the divisions of the first Epistle of St. John, would convince even the unlearned of the thoroughness of the work of these two great scholars.

In a letter written when he was a young man at Cambridge, Dr. Westcott set forth the idea of life which was ever present with him to the end. He said :

> " I should say that we live only so far as we cultivate all our faculties, and improve all our advantages for God's glory. The means of living then will be our endowments, whether of talent or influence ; the aim of living, the good of men ; the motive of living, the love of God."

APPENDICES

APPENDIX I

NOTES ON BISHOP WESTCOTT'S "*GOSPEL OF LIFE*" [1]

THE purpose of this inspiring book of deep thoughts and far-reaching hopes may be summed up in a single sentence. From the first page to the last it is written to show how in our Lord Jesus Christ we have the answer to all the mysteries of human life, the fulfilment of all its aspirations, and the solution to all the problems of ancient faiths and modern progress. The thoughts are thoughts for every Christian, and to grasp them in their full meaning is to gain fresh power both for study and for active work. But the form in which they are expressed, by closely reasoned arguments, is not always easy to follow without care and close attention. The aim, therefore, of these notes is to indicate their main outlines and deep practical interest, in the hope that some readers who can go no further may be able at least to make these central thoughts their own, and that others may be led on to the study of the book itself.

I. *The Mystery of Life*

Life is full of mysteries to every one who thinks at all. There are, first, our own selves—our longings and our

[1] Reprinted from *The Church Reading Magazine* for July 1903.

failures, the conflict of good and evil which we feel within us, and, above all, the impenetrable darkness before birth and after death. Then there is the world in which we live—other people, other nations, and the forces of nature, all influencing our individual lives so strongly, and yet so entirely beyond our understanding or control. And, last and greatest, there is the mystery of God—the unseen Power beyond and outside human will and effort, of which all men have been conscious from the earliest dawn of thought.

These mysteries are universal, and so is the longing to solve them. The various religions which we find in all the different regions of the earth are so many attempts at finding an answer that shall satisfy the soul. We are so apt to look upon religion as in some way responsible for the mysteries of life, that it is important to bear clearly in mind that it is the *answer* to them, not their *cause*.

Chapters I. and II. of *The Gospel of Life* deal with these foundation-facts of Christian thought; and Chapter III. defines the conditions under which any answer to these mysteries must be sought.

II. *Christianity the only true Answer to Life's Problems*

To these mysteries of life men have devised many answers; God has given only one, which is summed up in the Person of His Incarnate Son.

> "Christianity offers in a real human life the thoughts by which other religions live. . . . Truths which found fragmentary expression in præ-Christian religions are set before us in the Person and Work of the Lord, in His Birth and Passion and Resurrection and Ascension, so that all mysteries are brought together and reconciled in one mystery. In the Lord Jesus Christ, One Person, we see all things summed up . . . and united to God." (P. xxii.)

This point should be very clearly grasped before going

on to the question of spreading the Christian Faith, in
these days of compromises and confusing claims for a
divided sovereignty to be shared between Christianity,
Buddhism, Mohammedanism, and a host of other conflicting faiths. If Christianity is the *one* Faith it must
be the Faith *for all*; that is to say, it must be able to
meet the needs of every race and every man, and to
offer the satisfaction which millions at present seek in
other Creeds. And it can only do this by the old
Christlike method of fulfilling, not destroying. The aim
of the Christian should be not merely the destruction of
old and false beliefs, but the development of all that is
true in them to a more perfect fulfilment than can be
found except in Christ.

This is also a thought to be deeply pondered, and
brings us on to the third point.

III. *The Importance of Studying præ-Christian Faiths*

Chapter IV. deals with "the work of the præ-Christian
nations towards the solution of the problems of life,"
showing how in their blind gropings after a faith that
should satisfy men's restless strivings we have "the revelation of the soul's wants which the absolute religion must
meet." (P. 108.)

"Christianity—the Gospel of the Resurrection—is,
as I have already said, the complete answer to all our
questionings so far as we can receive an answer at
present—an answer which we are slowly spelling out
through the growing experience of the life of the
Church. But before this complete answer was given,
other answers were made, partial and tentative, which
offer for our study the most solemn aspect of ancient
history. . . . If we can in any way apprehend them
clearly, we shall understand better than by any other
method both the wants of man, and the resources
which he has himself for supplying them, and

the extent to which his natural endowments are able to satisfy his wants." (P. 94.)

IV. *The Ancient Book-Religions of the East*

Chapter V. deals with these, under the title of "Præ-Christian Gentile Solutions of the Problems of Being." The whole of this chapter should be studied by every reader desirous of understanding the relation of Christianity to other faiths. The deep, inner meaning of the Eastern book-religions—their *soul*, so to speak—is shown in a few words of marvellous insight; and the lines are indicated along which the outward forms and life of these religions may best be studied.

"... We must endeavour to keep in view the ruling thoughts of different systems; and at the very outset of our inquiry we may, I think, characterise by three words the three groups of præ-Christian Book-religions —the Turanian, the Aryan, the Shemitic—and such a characterisation will serve as a general clue to guide us as we go further. We may say with justice, speaking broadly, that the Chinese (Turanian) religions are impressed with the stamp of order, the Aryan with that of nature, and Shemitic with that of history." (P. 123.)

From this general survey the writer goes on to consider in more detail the distinctive features of the Chinese, Indian, and Persian Faiths. He shows how the two great Chinese leaders of thought, Lao-tzu and Confucius, strove to find the answer to life's mysteries, the one in the inner realm of mind and reason, the other in the outward order of things seen. Taouism preached an interior "way" of life, which the wise could find by thought and self-searching, and by which they could rise above, and even control, the outward course of circumstances. Confucianism dealt solely with the external order and relations of life; accepting these as necessarily good in themselves, and teaching

C. *On the Study of Special Subjects in the Bible*

Characteristics of the Gospel Miracles. (84-87.)

The Revelation of the Father. (75, 85, 88-90, 142, 197.)

The Revelation of the Risen Lord. (36-39, 85, 196, 197.)

The Gospel of the Resurrection. (33-37, 196.)

Christus Consummator. (18, 20, 173, 174, 198.)

D. *On Creed and Doctrine*

The Gospel of Life. (148, 229-235.)

The Historic Faith. (106-113.)

The Victory of the Cross. (46-58, 106.)

E. *On the Teaching of the Ordinal*

Some Thoughts from the Ordinal. (77.)

Gifts for Ministry. (119, 120.)

F. *Practical Helps in Daily Life*

Steps in the Christian Life. (9, 153, 134, 198.)

The Christian Life Manifold and One. (47.)

Common Prayers for Family Use. (12, 92.)

G. *On Social Questions*

Christian Social Union Addresses. (161.)

The Incarnation and Common Life. (29, 131-133, 148, 151-161, 176-183, 186, 188.)

Social Aspects of Christianity. (16, 96-100.)

H. *Miscellaneous Addresses* [1]

Christian Aspects of Life. (5, 17, 31, 32, 120-123, 125-130, 148, 183, 184, 188.)

---

[1] Some dealing with social, and some with spiritual questions.

Lessons from Work. (5, 65, 73, 74, 83, 90-92, 148, 187, 188.)

Words of Faith and Hope. (148, 161.)

Peterborough Sermons.

On Some Points in the Religious Office of the Universities. (76, 143-145.)

From Strength to Strength. (10, 22.)

I. *Historical and Literary Essays*

Essays in the History of Religious Thought in the West. (10.)

GENERAL INDEX[1]

Anxiety, 169
Atonement, the, 46-58

Benson, Archbishop, 172
Bible, nature of, 73; purpose of, 77, 78; revision of text, 82, 83
Bible study, importance of, 61-63; difficulties of, 64-72; hints on, 90
Boutflower, Archdeacon, 6

Cambridge, addresses to students, 7, 17
Christ (see Incarnation, Atonement, Resurrection)
Christian Social Union, 7, 161
Christian service, 181, 186
Church, the, 97, 101
Church services, value of, 118, 119; share of the congregation in, 120, 121; duty of studying, 122, 123
Congregation, responsibility of, 119-121
Co-operation, 161
Creed, the Christian, power of, 105, 106; meaning of, 106, 107; necessity for, 111, 187

Doctrine, definition of, 28

Education, 15, 183
Empire, the Roman, 101-103
Enthusiasm, 187

Faith, definitions of, 107-109; plea for open confession of Faith, 178, 187
Fellowship, 131, 135, 153
Foreign Missions, 137-148
Forgiveness, 56
Formulas, nature of, 27

Gambling, 154
Glory of God, 17, 75
God (see Glory and Presence)
Gospels, nature of, 71; study of, 83, 84

Holy Communion, 124
Holy Spirit, the, as the Spirit of Christ, 42; as a power in daily life, 43, 44, 180
Hort, Dr., 10, 198

Ideals, the power of, 5, 187
Incarnation, the, 20, 29-32, 152
"In Christ," force of the phrase, 30-32, 82, 142

Kingdom of God, 63, 96-104, 183

Labour, 161, 177
Leisure, use of, 182
Life, Christian, 21, 22, 179
Lightfoot, Bishop, 10, 171
Loss, 170-172
Love, power of, 168, 173
Luxury, 157, 158

[1] This index does not include references to any of Bishop Westcott's books, as these are given separately in Appendix II.

THE END

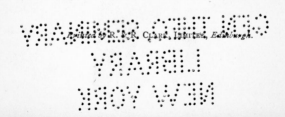
Printed by R. & R. CLARK, LIMITED, *Edinburgh.*